Risotto
'round the world!

TAMARA MILSTEIN

Author's Acknowledgements

*Special thanks to my wonderfully supportive husband, Kevin,
who has been tireless in his encouragement and enthusiasm for all that I do.*

*To my five children, who happily kiss me good-bye as I leave
to teach yet another class, thank you for understanding.*

*Thank you Mum, for always being there when I need you to help out
with the children, the dishes, the mail, and a hundred other tasks.*

*Last but not least, thanks to Jennifer Oliver and Richard Carroll for
your professional encouragement, assistance and enthusiasm.*

MAJOR CREDITS
Published by:
R&R Publications Marketing Pty Ltd
(ACN 083 612 579)
PO Box 254 Carlton North
Victoria 3054
National Toll Free: 1 800 063 296
© Richard Carroll
Publisher: Richard Carroll
Author: Tamara Milstein
Computer Manager: Sean McNamara
Creative Director: Jon Terpstra
Photographer: Mark O'Meara
Food Stylist: Stephane Souvlis
Assistant: Jenny Fanshaw
Proof Reader: Victoria Rowlands

The National Library of Australia
Cataloguing-in-Publication Data

Milstein, Tamara, 1965- .
  Risotto 'round the world
  Bibliography.
  Includes index.
  ISBN: 1 875655 68 9
  1. Cookery (Rice). 2. Risotto. 1. Title
641.6318

First printed October 1996
Second edition printed April 1997
Third edition printed October 1997
Fourth edition printed October 1998
This edition printed November 1999

Computer typeset in Optima and Monotype Script Bold by:
R&R Publications Marketing Pty Ltd, Carlton North, VIC, Australia
Film Scanning: PICA Overseas, Singapore
Printed by: APP Printing, Singapore

The publishers would like to acknowledge and thank the following
contributors for their support and assistance with the provision of materials
for photography, and food for photography and recipe development:

Accoutrement, Mosman and Woollahra, NSW
Home and Gardens, Sky Gardens, Sydney, NSW
Hugh Webb Antiques, East Sydney, NSW
Valcorp Holdings Pty Ltd, Richmond, VIC
Villeroy & Boch, Brookvale, NSW

Contents

Introduction

Risotto is certainly a dish of the nineties. Its elevation from simple, peasant meal in Italy's north to dinner tables in the best restaurants in New York, London and other great cities is not surprising. It can be found in a multitude of flavours, with ingredients as simple as a few freshly picked herbs or as elaborate as truffles and caviar; it can be found on elegant restaurant menus, scrawled on blackboards in busy bistros, on family dinner tables or crumbed and fried in my children's lunchboxes. Risotto has only one vice—it must be cooked correctly! A risotto that is incorrectly prepared will never develop a wonderful creamy consistency with each grain of rice remaining 'al dente', nor will the flavours sing with freshness from the depths of this starch-based dish. Correctly cooked, a risotto is simply—Heaven!

The basic ingredients are simple and readily available, the flavours can be adapted to suit the palate of the diner, rice is nutritious and wholesome, and the cooking is easy—all the ingredients for a perfect nineties dish.

When beginning research for this book, I forced my memory back to my first risotto—a saffron-based speciality of Milan called, appropriately, Risotto alla Milanese. My first taste of risotto was in a little restaurant in Milan, on a blustery winter afternoon, with shopping bags at my feet and a waiter who called me 'bella' and who drew a heart in my cappuccino—little wonder that everything that day was perfect. My love affair with risotto began that day, about ten years ago, and continues today with as much gusto as ever. I order it everywhere I have the opportunity—my eyes drawn instinctively to the place on the menu where risotto beckons. I have been delighted by the simplicity of risotto with tomato and basil, seduced by risotto with smoked salmon, caviar or fresh porcini mushrooms and inspired by such unusual ingredients as strawberries and champagne.

My motivation for writing this book is a desire to 'spread the word'. Risotto is the most requested recipe in my cooking school and on radio, and after three years of teaching risotto cookery I see no decline in its popularity by its devotees. After fine-tuning recipes for traditional risotto, I began to experiment with an eclectic mix of ingredients and, to my delight, I found that this style of cooking rice lends itself to almost any flavour. Imagine a risotto with Greek-style lamb, enhanced with lemon, rosemary and yoghurt, or a satay-flavoured dish featuring chicken, peanuts, sesame oil and green onions. These and many more unusual combinations feature in this book.

Also included is a selection of low fat risotto. I firmly believe that risotto can feature admirably in a low fat diet, and after tasting a risotto of mixed cherry tomatoes or Risotto Niçoise— my own creation of fresh tuna, beans, potato and olives—I am sure you will agree.

Never-before published is a selection of risotto perfect for desserts. Containing fruits, nuts and liquor, they really do confirm that this style of cooking is just so adaptable. I had a wonderful time introducing my friends and acquaintances to these new selections, and I am sure that you will enjoy eating and serving them too.

Finally, what to do with leftover risotto (if you ever have any left over)? I have included several simply perfect solutions to using leftover risotto. They work so well that you may find yourself making extra, just so you have some left over to create Arrancini, Risotto al Salto or an innovative pie or quiche crust.

I hope you will imbibe some of my passion for this wonderfully adaptable dish, and that these recipes will assist you in making risotto your personal favourite too.

Happy stirring!

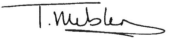

Tamara Milstein

The Basics

*W*ithout doubt, Risotto is my favourite Italian dish. When cooked correctly it is creamy, moist and flavourful. When cooked incorrectly it can be gluggy, dry and uninteresting. Risotto is so easy to make once you understand a few basic rules, and yet it is amazing how many people cannot seem to make a good risotto. Following the instructions below you will never go wrong, and soon you will be able to add your own favourite flavours to create dishes of your own.

*T*here are several very important rules to follow when making risotto. None of these is difficult or unusual but if the rules are not followed correctly, the risotto will never be perfect.

1. The broth or stock must always be simmering before being added to the rice. If the stock is not hot, the temperature of the rice will continuously cool, which will make the rice gluggy and very slow to cook. The easiest way to do this is to have the stock simmering in a small saucepan next to the risotto so that you can add it as it is needed.

2. The broth must be added ladle by ladle. If it is added too quickly, the rice will absorb the liquid quickly and not be able to develop the creamy texture for which risotto is famous.

3. When cooking the onion (and garlic), be sure to cook only until the onion is transparent, not browned. Browning the onion will impart a bitter flavour which will dull the other flavours present in the dish.

4. Stir the risotto frequently during cooking. The more stirring, the creamier the texture. Stirring forces each grain of rice to rub against another, loosening the starch which is required to create a starchy, creamy texture; so the more you stir, the creamier the rice.

5. When all the liquid has all been added, turn off the heat immediately. If you continue to cook the risotto it will be too dry. As soon as the heat has been turned off, add the butter,

cream, cheese or any other final flavouring and stir these through to incorporate. Serve immediately.

6. **Never wash the rice**. The texture for which arborio rice is famous is a result of the starch on the surface of each grain—if you wash off the starch it will never develop a creamy texture.

7. Always serve risotto as soon as it is cooked. Risotto waits for no man. I prefer to wait for my guests to arrive before I begin to cook.

Short Cuts

*I*f you find that time is short and risotto is difficult to make with your busy lifestyle, you may like to adopt one of the following suggestions.

1. Most risotto can be prepared up to the point where you add the stock, with no loss of flavour. Simply heat oil or butter, add onion/garlic etc., add wine and allow to be absorbed, then cease cooking. This will cut about ten minutes off your cooking time. When continuing the risotto later in the day, add the first ladle of boiling stock and stir well to break up the rice mass, then continue as per your recipe.

2. If using arborio rice, all the stock may be added at one time, once the wine has been absorbed. Simply add all the hot stock, stir well and cover the saucepan with a lid, reducing the heat to low. Cook for 8-10 minutes and stir well again. Finish with cream, cheese etc. and serve. Risotto cooked this way will have slightly softer grains than the traditional risotto, because the rice is steaming as well as simmering. Nevertheless, this is the perfect solution for a nineties cook who lacks sufficient time.

Note

*A*ll recipes in this book have been developed to serve four adults.

Traditional Italian Flavours

*I*t is because of the flavours in this chapter that I first embarked on a love affair with risotto.

*M*y first taste of risotto has stayed with me and has, to a certain extent, shaped the direction in which my teaching has developed. These recipes all remain true to the flavours of the traditional Italian kitchen and are a wonderful stepping stone into this extensive range of flavour combinations.

*W*hether you begin with a simple, summery risotto of fresh tomatoes and basil, or an elegant combination of spinach and Gorgonzola, you will be rewarded with a delicious and enticing blend of flavours.

*T*here are recipes in this chapter to suit all tastes and all seasons—a risotto of porcini mushrooms is an autumn treat hard to match, while the combination of veal and sage will warm the heart and stomach on the coldest winter day.

*I*t is with these recipes that I begin to share with you my passion for a simple, peasant dish.

*J*oin with me in celebrating tradition.

Risotto with Saffron and Peas

Risotto Milanese

My first taste of risotto was of this Milanese speciality and it remains my personal favourite. Saffron can be purchased in powdered form or threads, but since the powder has often been bulked with fillers, I prefer to use saffron threads. Use a mortar and pestle to crush the threads to get the most flavour and colour out of these dried stamens of the crocus flower. Saffron can be purchased from good delicatessens and food stores. It has an unlimited shelf life.

Ingredients

1 tablespoon olive oil
1 tablespoon butter
1 clove garlic, minced
1 medium white onion, minced or finely chopped
400g arborio rice
125ml dry white wine
900ml rich vegetable or chicken stock, simmering
½ teaspoon saffron threads
1 cup fresh garden peas
1 tablespoon mascarpone cheese
2 tablespoons Parmesan cheese, grated
lots of fresh parsley and ground black pepper to serve

Method

Add the saffron to the hot stock and rest until required.

Heat the olive oil and butter, and sauté the garlic and white onion until softened. Add the rice and stir to coat. Add the wine and allow it to be absorbed. Add the first addition of stock, stirring well and allowing it to be absorbed before the next addition of stock. Continue adding stock, half a cup at a time and stirring well between each addition.

When adding the last addition of stock, add the garden peas and cook for 2 minutes, or until almost all the liquid has been absorbed.

Remove the risotto from the heat. Add the mascarpone and grated Parmesan cheeses and plenty of parsley and black pepper. Serve immediately.

Variation—Traditional Risotto Milanese with Bone Marrow

Risotto Milanese usually contains bone marrow which can easily be extracted from shank bones, cut in half by your butcher. Following the trend toward lighter cooking, many restaurants now omit this step; but if you should wish to include it, simply extract about 1 tablespoon and sauté it with the onions. The marrow will break up and change colour when cooked. Continue with the recipe as above. The addition of bone marrow creates a wonderful rich and smooth flavour.

Risotto of Tomato and Basil
Risotto Pomodori e Basilico

(photographed on page 9)

This risotto sings of summer. Its flavours are light and refreshing and the ingredients are easy to find. If you have a vegetable garden, stroll down and pluck a few tomatoes and a handful of fresh basil leaves. You'll have dinner on the table in an instant!

Ingredients

1 tablespoon butter
1 tablespoon olive oil
2 cloves garlic, minced
1 finely chopped onion
400g arborio rice
125ml dry white wine
900ml vegetable or chicken stock, simmering
4 roma tomatoes, chopped into large dice
8 La Gina sun-dried tomatoes
20 fresh basil leaves, cut into strips
$\frac{1}{3}$ cup grated Parmesan cheese
2 tablespoons mascarpone cheese

Method

Heat the butter and oil in a large saucepan and add the garlic and onion. Sauté until the onion is transparent. Add the rice and stir to coat. Add the wine and stir well, allowing the wine to be absorbed before adding any more liquid.

Begin adding the stock a ladle at a time, allowing each addition to be absorbed before adding the next ladle of stock. Remember to stir the risotto intermittently throughout the cooking time.

When half the stock has been absorbed, add the tomatoes, chopped sun-dried tomatoes and the basil, and stir well. Continue to add stock until the rice is still firm to bite and all the liquid has been absorbed.

Remove the saucepan from the heat immediately and stir through the Parmesan and mascarpone cheeses and freshly ground salt and pepper to taste.

Garnish with extra fresh basil leaves and serve immediately.

Variation—Risotto of Tomato and Chicken (Risotto Pomodori e Pollo)

The addition of a simple poached chicken breast, shredded into bite-size pieces, makes a lovely change. Simply purchase a skinless, boneless breast of chicken and poach over simmering water for 10 minutes, or until cooked through. Cool then shred. Add to the risotto when adding the tomatoes, then continue as above.

Risotto with Fresh Herbs

Risotto all'erbe

I love to serve this pretty green risotto as an appetiser. It is light, fresh and full of the flavours of a summer garden. It also makes a perfect accompaniment to roast chicken or lamb.

Ingredients

2 tablespoons light olive oil
10 spring onions, chopped
400g arborio rice
125ml white wine
900ml vegetable stock, simmering
½ cup fresh dill, ½ cup fresh parsley, ½ cup fresh basil,
½ cup fresh chives, or 2 cups fresh herbs of your choice
2 tablespoons sour cream
3 tablespoons grated Parmesan cheese
assorted fresh herb sprigs to garnish

Method

Heat the olive oil in a large saucepan and add the spring onions. Cook gently until the onions are softened. Add the rice and stir well to toast. Add the wine and stir until the wine has been absorbed.

Begin adding the stock a ladle at a time, allowing each addition to be absorbed before adding the next ladle of stock. Remember to stir the risotto intermittently throughout the cooking time. After the second addition of stock, add all the herbs and continue stirring.

When all the stock has been added and absorbed, remove the pan from heat immediately.

Add the sour cream and grated Parmesan cheese.

Garnish with fresh herb sprigs and serve immediately.

Variation—Risotto of White Fish and Fresh Herbs

To make this dish a little more substantial, I like to add some white fish fillets. Purchase 400g Sea Perch or Blue Eye and cut into cubes. Add to the risotto with the spring onions and stir until the fish is opaque. Remove the fish and keep warm. Continue making the risotto as above, adding the cooked fish with the last addition of stock.

Risotto with Porcini Mushrooms
Risotto con Funghi Porcini

This risotto has a very earthy flavour and is delicious using any mushrooms. There are so many fresh varieties on the market, you could combine two or three of these with the dried porcini, or just use the ingredients specified here.

Ingredients

30g dried porcini mushrooms
3 cups boiling water
2 tablespoons olive oil
1 tablespoon butter
1 medium leek, white part only, and sliced
½ cup chopped Italian parsley
1 large clove garlic, minced, or 1½ teaspoons minced garlic
2 cups arborio rice
750ml boiling beef or veal stock
125ml red wine
2 tablespoons tomato paste
250g assorted forest mushrooms, Swiss brown, shiitake, oyster, portobello, etc.
½ cup freshly grated Parmesan cheese
3 tablespoons minced parsley

Method

Soak the porcini mushrooms in the boiling water for at least half an hour. Carefully clean the soaked mushrooms and chop, discarding stems. Strain the mushroom liquid carefully through several layers of paper towels or muslin to remove grit and sand. Reserve this mushroom stock for later use.

Meanwhile, finely chop the leek, parsley and garlic, and sauté in the olive oil and butter until transparent.

Add the rice, stir to coat then add the wine and stir until evaporated. Add the soaked mushrooms, tomato paste and the fresh sliced mushrooms. Mix the mushroom liquid with the boiling stock and begin to add stock mixture to the rice one ladle at a time, allowing each ladle of stock to be absorbed before the next one is added, and stirring well.

When liquid is used and rice is still firm to bite, remove from heat, add Parmesan cheese and extra parsley and serve immediately.

Risotto with Spinach and Gorgonzola

Risotto Spinaci e Gorgonzola

This risotto is quite rich and would be perfect for an entrée or a light lunch, served with a green salad. For those who do not like blue cheese, simply substitute a mild brie or soft goat's cheese.

Ingredients

2 tablespoons olive oil

2 cloves garlic, minced, or 2 teaspoons minced garlic

1 onion, finely chopped

400g arborio rice

400g spinach, cooked and chopped, or 1 pack frozen spinach

2 handfuls washed baby spinach leaves

1 litre vegetable stock

250g Gorgonzola dolce latte (mild, sweet Gorgonzola)

freshly ground pepper to taste

fresh parsley or chives to garnish

Method

Bring the stock to simmer and set aside.

Sauté the onion and garlic in the olive oil and cook briefly until transparent. Add the rice and stir to coat. Add the chopped fresh or frozen spinach and one ladle of stock, and stir well, ensuring that the spinach is well distributed.

Continue adding stock in the usual manner until the liquid has been added. Add the baby spinach leaves and the Gorgonzola, cut into small pieces and stir to combine. Allow to sit for a minute or two so that the cheese can melt. Stir once more and serve immediately, garnished with some chopped fresh parsley or chives and plenty of freshly ground black pepper.

Serve immediately.

Risotto with Pumpkin

Risotto con Zucca

This deliciously creamy risotto can be made with any variety of pumpkin, but I prefer to use butternut which is quite sweet and very soft in texture. It is important to add half the pumpkin in raw cubes and half which has been pre-cooked and mashed, to achieve a bright golden coloured dish with plenty of texture.

Ingredients

1 large butternut pumpkin, cut into large chunks
1 tablespoon butter
1 tablespoon oil
1 large Spanish (red) onion, finely diced
400g arborio rice
300ml dry white wine
800ml vegetable stock
1 tablespoon lemon juice
$\frac{1}{3}$ cup chopped parsley
$\frac{1}{3}$ cup Parmesan cheese
1-2 tablespoons mascarpone cheese, to finish

Method

Before beginning the risotto, boil half the pumpkin chunks until very soft, drain and mash, seasoning with salt and pepper to taste. Set aside.

Heat the oil and butter and gently fry the onion until soft. Add the remaining chunks of raw pumpkin and cook for 5 minutes. Add the rice and toast briefly. Add the white wine and allow the rice to absorb it. Begin adding the stock, a cup at a time, and stirring well with each addition.

When half the stock has been absorbed, add the pumpkin purée and continue cooking the risotto, adding stock as necessary. When the stock has all been absorbed, add the lemon juice, Parmesan and parsley and stir well. Add the mascarpone, stir to combine, sprinkle with extra parsley if desired, and serve.

Variation—Risotto with Pumpkin and Lamb (Risotto con Zucca e Agnello)

Although not Italian, roast lamb is a perfect addition to this risotto. I like to reserve leftover roast lamb, cut into chunks, and freeze for later use. When I make pumpkin risotto, I simply defrost a tub or two of lamb and add it to the risotto, half way through the cooking time, with the mashed pumpkin.

Risotto with Seafood and Tomato

Risotto Marinara

Risotto is a perfect vehicle for serving shellfish. The liquid stock helps to keep the seafood moist and tender, while allowing the seafood to impart its lovely briny flavours. I like to cook the seafood briefly before beginning the risotto to ensure even cooking of the fish, and also to avoid the risk of over-cooking. The seafood is then added with the last addition of stock. If the specified seafoods are not available, simply use other varieties of your choice that equal the same weight. Although not regarded as etiquette, I like to add a little Parmesan cheese with seafood; if you prefer to not to, simply leave it out.

Ingredients

1 tablespoon olive oil
2 cloves garlic, minced
200g calamari, washed and cut into rings
200g raw green prawns, heads and shells removed
200g fillet of fresh Atlantic salmon, skin removed, cut into bite-sized pieces, or sliced thinly
½ cup minced parsley

1 tablespoon olive oil
10 spring onions, chopped

400g arborio rice
300ml dry white wine
800ml rich fish stock, simmering
4 roma tomatoes, finely chopped

1 tablespoon sour cream
2 tablespoons grated Parmesan cheese
½ cup finely chopped parsley

Method

Heat the olive oil and gently sauté the garlic. Add the prepared seafood and cook briefly until the fish and shellfish is opaque, adding the parsley at the last moment. Remove from heat and set aside.

Heat the remaining tablespoon of olive oil and sauté the spring onions. Add the rice, stirring to coat. Add the white wine and allow it to be absorbed, then add the first addition of fish stock together with the finely chopped tomatoes. Continue cooking, adding further additions of stock as the previous one is absorbed.

When there is only a small quantity of stock left, add the cooked fish mixture and all its juices with the last addition of stock and continue simmering for about 2 minutes, or until most of the liquid is absorbed. Add sour cream, cheese and parsley, stir well to incorporate and serve immediately.

Tuscan Risotto
with Artichoke, Capsicum and Fontina

This risotto really does remind me of Tuscany. The flavours of roasted artichokes, sun-dried tomatoes and capsicums are simply stunning when cooked in risotto. The slow cooking of the rice allows the flavours of the preserved vegetables to be imparted and then absorbed by the rice. Any other roasted vegetables can be added, such as eggplant or perhaps olives, but I like it just like this. Fontina is a wonderful soft yellow cheese, from Piedmont, which enriches all the foods with which it is cooked. Similar to a Swiss râclette, it melts beautifully and will not become stringy or tough.

Ingredients

2 tablespoons olive oil (from preserved vegetables if possible)
1 leek, cleaned and chopped
6 shallots, finely chopped
3 garlic cloves, minced

400g arborio rice
200ml white wine
800ml rich vegetable stock
10 sun-dried tomatoes (in oil, drained)
4 sun-dried capsicums (in oil, drained)
4 roasted artichokes, drained and sliced or quartered

10 fresh basil leaves, finely shredded
½ cup grated Fontina cheese

2 tablespoons Parmesan cheese
extra basil leaves to garnish

Method

Heat the olive oil and sauté the leek, shallots and garlic until softened, about 5 minutes.

Add the rice and stir to coat the rice, then add the wine and allow to be absorbed. Begin adding the stock, half a cup at a time, stirring well after each addition. When half the stock has been absorbed, add the sun-dried tomatoes, capsicums and artichokes and continue adding stock as required, stirring.

With the last addition of stock, add the basil and Fontina and cook for 2 minutes more. Remove the risotto from the heat and stir very well. Garnish with extra basil leaves and Parmesan cheese and serve immediately.

Variation—Risotto with Preserved Vegetables and Rabbit

One of the most popular meats in Tuscany is rabbit. It is inexpensive and has a good, rich flavour. Rabbit fillets pair well with the strong flavours of vegetables preserved in oil and make a nice change for those who enjoy meat. The addition of rabbit will also make this dish much more hearty, requiring only a green salad and some good bread for a well rounded meal.

Purchase 500g rabbit fillets, and dice. Add to the risotto with the leek/shallot mixture and cook until the meat changes colour. Continue with the risotto as above.

Risotto with Veal and Sage
Risotto con Vitello e Salvia

This risotto has a very earthy flavour and is deliciously rich and flavoursome. I like to buy ready-diced veal for convenience and fresh sage leaves are a must! Although this risotto can be made with vegetable or chicken stock, using veal stock will really enhance the flavours of this winter dish. To make easy veal stock, purchase 1kg of veal bones and roast in the oven at 250°C for 1 hour. Add these to 1 litre of ready-prepared beef stock with 2 cups of water. Bring to the boil and simmer for 1 hour. Taste for seasoning.

Ingredients

2 tablespoons butter or olive oil
350g veal, cut into cubes
2 tablespoons tomato paste
3 tablespoons minced parsley
½ cup fresh sage leaves, tightly packed, chopped
2 tablespoons olive oil
1 medium leek
2 cloves garlic, minced
2 cups arborio rice
200ml red wine such as Chianti
1½ litres boiling beef or veal stock
½ cup chopped Italian parsley
½ cup grated Parmesan cheese, to serve
crispy fried sage leaves to garnish (about 1 bunch)

Method

In a sauté pan, heat the olive oil or butter until very hot and add the cubed veal. Cook quickly until the meat changes colour, then add the tomato paste, sage and parsley. Cook for 2 more minutes until the meat is well cooked, then allow to cool.

In a separate pot, heat the remaining 2 tablespoons olive oil. Add the garlic and leek and sauté until the vegetables are softened. Add the rice, stir to coat then add the wine and stir until evaporated.

Begin to add the simmering stock one ladle at a time, allowing each ladle of stock to be absorbed before the next one is added. When half the stock has been incorporated, continue adding stock in the same fashion until it has all been used. When all the liquid is added and the rice is still firm to bite, remove from heat, add Parmesan cheese, extra parsley and veal mixture and serve immediately over a small pile of crispy sage leaves.

Note

To fry sage leaves, simply heat a little oil until smoking and add sage leaves a few at a time. When they cease sizzling, remove from the oil with a slotted spoon and drain on absorbent paper.

Variation

Veal may be added to the stock and rice mixture during cooking if desired.

Risotto with Smoked Salmon

Risotto con Salmone Affumicato

This deliciously rich risotto is certainly one to save for special occasions or when you want to impress somebody. I like to add lemon zest and juice to reduce the richness, and a little cream to create a silky texture. I serve this risotto with a garnish of black and red caviar which looks stunning, but do not add the caviar until you are taking the risotto to the table, as it tends to 'bleed'.

Ingredients

2 tablespoons olive oil
1 Spanish (red) onion
2 cloves garlic, minced
2 tablespoons fresh dill
zest of 1 large lemon

400g arborio rice
200ml white wine
900ml good quality light fish stock (or vegetable)

100ml fresh cream
200g excellent quality smoked salmon
juice of 1 lemon
½ bunch of chives
½ cup Parmesan cheese

2 tablespoons black caviar
2 tablespoons red caviar

Method

Heat the olive oil and sauté the garlic and onion until softened. Add the dill and zest of lemon and sauté 1 minute further, until the fragrance of the herb and lemon are distinct. Add the rice and stir to coat, then add the wine and continue to cook until absorbed, about 3 minutes.

Begin adding the stock, half a cup at a time and stir well between each addition. When each quantity has been absorbed, add the next addition of stock. When all the stock has been used and incorporated, remove the pan from the heat.

Add the cream, lemon, chives, Parmesan and smoked salmon which has been cut into thin strips. Stir well and allow to sit for 2 minutes to allow the flavours to blend and the liquid to be partially absorbed.

Spoon into individual bowls and garnish with a spoonful each of red and black caviar. Serve immediately.

Mediterranean Influence

*T*he influence of the Mediterranean has had a profound effect on me and my style of cooking.

*O*nce I understood risotto, I wanted more. More flavours, more ideas, more choice.

I looked to the areas around Italy for this diversity because the climate and the vegetation have many similarities and therefore, many existing flavour combinations.

*T*he more I experimented, the more confident I became. What started out as a lamb souvlaki, became a risotto of Greek flavours—a gem of a dish full of lemon-spiked lamb, rosemary and garlic. While not at all Italian, the flavours worked beautifully with the rice, and the more I shared these ideas, the more enthusiastic I became.

A large amount of leftover roasted garlic became the inspiration for another risotto; some quail with Moroccan spices eventually made its way into another new recipe.

*Y*ou can see how easy it is to be swept along by a tide of new flavours, all shining in their own way.

*I*magine a cobalt blue sky, a bright yellow sun and the red, red earth. Now that you are in the Mediterranean, cook up a treat!

Risotto of Roasted Garlic

This wonderful dish was created quite by chance. I had lots of leftover roasted garlic from a Mediterranean cooking class I was teaching, and simply could not throw it away. As often happens when I am too tired to cook or go out and I crave risotto, I cook. So I made a simple risotto with no particularly strong flavours, and then towards the end I tossed in the roasted garlic. The wonderful flavours and aromas mingled and helped to create this sublime dish.

Ingredients

2 heads of garlic
1 tablespoon olive oil
1½ tablespoons olive oil
2 medium brown onions

400g arborio rice
200ml white wine
900ml rich vegetable stock, simmering

1 cup parsley, chopped
1 tablespoon mascarpone cheese
½ cup Parmesan cheese
freshly ground black pepper

Method

First prepare the garlic. Separate and peel all the cloves of garlic and toss with the olive oil. Place in an ovenproof baking dish and roast at 220°C for 30 minutes or until garlic is golden and sizzling. Do not allow them to brown which will create a bitter burnt flavour. Remove from the oven and cool.

Heat the second quantity of olive oil in a saucepan and add the chopped brown onions. Sauté briefly until they are translucent but not browned, then add the rice and stir to coat. Add the wine and allow to cook, stirring all the time, until the wine has been absorbed.

Begin adding the stock, a ladle at a time and stirring well after each addition. When half the stock has been added, add all but 8 cloves of garlic and stir to incorporate. Continue adding stock in the usual manner until all has been added and the rice is still firm to bite. Immediately remove the risotto from the heat and add the mascarpone cheese, half the parsley and half the grated Parmesan. Stir vigorously to incorporate all the ingredients then serve in individual bowls. Garnish with remaining garlic cloves that have been sliced or chopped, remaining Parmesan cheese, parsley and pepper.

Variation

I adore the marriage of garlic and eggplant, so I now often make this risotto with both. Simply buy 2 medium eggplants and chop into small dice. Sprinkle with salt and allow the bitter juices to drain. Wash briefly and dry well. Toss the eggplant with the raw garlic cloves and roast in the oven as described above. Add all the eggplant/garlic mixture (reserve 8 garlic cloves) to the risotto halfway through the cooking process and proceed as above. Garnish and serve.

Risotto of Greek Flavours

(photographed on page 29)

This wonderfully-flavoured risotto is both rich and light at the same time. The lemon and rosemary marinated lamb is best marinated for at least an hour to develop a true Greek flavour. The lamb really imparts its flavour to the rice which is both well textured and creamy at the same time.

Ingredients

400g lean lamb fillets cut into long strips
juice of two lemons
2 garlic cloves, minced
2 tablespoons fresh rosemary spikes
2 tablespoons olive oil

1 tablespoon olive oil
1 large onion, chopped roughly

400g arborio rice
200ml dry white wine
850ml chicken stock

1 cup parsley, chopped
½ cup Greek yoghurt
2 tablespoons Parmesan cheese

extra Greek yoghurt to garnish

Method

In a large non-reactive container, mix lamb, lemon juice, garlic, rosemary spikes and olive oil. Allow to marinate for at least hour or as long as 6 hours.

Heat the remaining olive oil in a saucepan and add the onion. Sauté until softened and then add the lamb mixture. Cook until the lamb changes colour and the onion is golden, about 5 minutes. Add the rice and stir to coat. Add the wine and continue cooking until the liquid has been absorbed.

Begin adding the stock, ½ a cup at a time, stirring well and allowing the liquid to absorb before adding the next quantity of stock. When all the stock has been absorbed, remove the risotto from the heat and add the parsley, Greek yoghurt and Parmesan cheese. Stir well to combine and serve immediately with a dollop of extra yoghurt if desired.

Variation—Greek Chicken Risotto

This risotto works equally well with chicken. Simply use the equivalent weight of chicken meat, either breast or thigh, cut into cubes and proceed with the recipe as above.

Risotto of Roasted Vegetables with Pesto

I make a roasted vegetable pizza which inspired me to create this dish. It is really very easy but always draws rave reviews because of the wonderful flavours of roasted Italian vegetables. If any of the vegetables called for are unavailable, simply use another. A spoonful of fresh pesto when serving elevates this dish from simply delicious to stunning!

Ingredients

1 large Spanish onion
1 red capsicum
1 yellow capsicum
1 small eggplant
1 bunch of asparagus
2 tablespoons olive oil

1 tablespoon olive oil
2 cloves garlic, minced
4 spring onions, chopped

400g arborio rice
200ml white wine
850ml vegetable stock

50g Parmesan cheese
2 tablespoons sour cream
freshly ground black pepper

Method

Dice the eggplant and sprinkle with salt. Allow the eggplant to drain for 30 minutes then rinse briefly and dry well. Peel and quarter the onion, remove the seeds from the capsicums and cut the flesh into large chunks. Cut away tough stalks from asparagus and cut into manageable lengths. Mix all these vegetables with the olive oil and roast at 240°C for 30 minutes, stirring once.

Meanwhile, begin the risotto. Heat the remaining olive oil and add the garlic and spring onions. Add the rice and stir to coat. Add the white wine and allow the liquid to be absorbed. Begin adding stock, half a cup at a time and stir well between each addition.

When adding the last addition of stock, add the roasted vegetables and their juice and stir to combine.

Add the grated cheese, sour cream and black pepper and serve immediately with a spoonful of pesto on top.

Note

To make pesto, process 2 cups tightly packed basil leaves, 2 cloves garlic, ½ cup toasted pine nuts and ½ cup grated Parmesan cheese. With the motor running, add enough olive oil to reach the consistency you desire, about ¾ cup is usually enough for a firm pesto. Pour a little olive oil over the surface and chill until required.

Risotto Tricolour
with Red, Yellow and Green Capsicums

I love this risotto. It is bright, happy and full of flavour and the ingredients are those I usually have in the fridge and pantry. If you are lucky enough to find orange peppers, use them too.

Ingredients

2 tablespoons olive oil
2 red capsicums
2 yellow capsicums
2 green capsicums
4 cloves garlic, minced
400g arborio rice
150ml dry white wine
900ml vegetable stock
2 tablespoons butter, mascarpone or cream
$\frac{1}{2}$ cup parsley
freshly ground pepper to serve

Method

Remove the seed core from each capsicum and discard. Cut the flesh into strips about 5mm thick.

Heat 2 tablespoons olive oil in a saucepan and sauté the garlic gently. Add the capsicums and continue cooking for 5 minutes. Add the rice and stir to coat. Add the wine and allow all the liquid to be absorbed.

Begin adding the stock, half a cup at a time, stirring well after each addition and allowing all the liquid to be thoroughly absorbed before adding the next quantity of stock.

When all the stock has been added, remove the risotto from the heat and add the butter, mascarpone or cream, parsley and black pepper to taste. Stir well and serve immediately.

Variation—Risotto with Mixed Peppers and Prawns

Somehow the flavour of prawns and mixed peppers pairs perfectly well together. It is a particularly unusual combination and yet it is just delicious. Sauté 12 raw, peeled prawns with the garlic and when cooked, remove and keep warm. Add the peppers and continue the recipe as above. Return the prawns to the risotto with the final addition of stock and finish as specified.

Moroccan Quail Risotto

This risotto dish has all the flavours and aromas of Morocco. The spiced quail is really delicious and can be added to the risotto or roasted separately (see note). The Middle Eastern influence is continued with the addition of currants and pine nuts and the cinnamon stick, cumin and turmeric all contribute to an intensely flavoured, heart-warming meal.

Ingredients

2 tablespoons olive oil
1 teaspoon ground cumin
1 teaspoon ground coriander
1 teaspoon turmeric
1 cinnamon stick
2 leeks, white part only, washed and sliced finely
650g quail—legs, breast or mixture
(or 400g quail meat off the bone)
400g arborio rice
200ml light red (or white) wine
800ml rich chicken or turkey stock
½ cup currants
½ cup parsley
⅓ cup pine nuts, toasted
1 leek extra, white part only
oil for frying
freshly ground black pepper

Method

Heat the olive oil in a large saucepan and add the spices and cinnamon stick. Stir gently to release the aroma, then add the leek. Sauté until softened and add the quail pieces. Sauté gently to seal in the juices of the quail and allow all the wonderful flavours to blend, about 10 minutes. Do not cook at a high heat because the spices will burn, imparting a bitter flavour.

Remove the quail pieces and transfer to a roasting pan. Cover with foil and bake for 15-20 minutes or until cooked. Meanwhile continue the risotto. To the remaining spices and leek in the pan, add the rice and stir to coat. Add the wine and allow the liquid to be absorbed. Begin to add the stock, half a cup at a time, stirring well after each addition. Add the currants with the second addition of stock and continue adding liquid and stirring in the usual manner. With the last addition of stock, add the parsley and cook for 2 minutes. Remove from heat. Shred some roasted quail from the bone and mix into the risotto, leaving 1 or 2 attractive pieces of quail whole for each person (I like to save the leg pieces). Remove the cinnamon stick.

Spoon the risotto into individual bowls and garnish with the quail, pine nuts, pepper and deep fried leek. Serve immediately.

Note

The quail can be totally shredded if you prefer, after roasting, and added to the risotto with the last addition of stock.

To deep fry the leek, wash and cut the white part into long thin strips. Heat some oil to 190°C then add the leek strips all at once. With a spoon, swish them around in the oil and when golden, lift with a slotted spoon, allow to drain on absorbent paper then serve as a garnish on the risotto.

Fresh Beetroot Risotto

This is a risotto to impress! The bright pink colour, topped off with orange sweet potato chips, will combine to create a dish worthy of the most elegant dinner party. Serve this risotto as an entrée only, rather than a main course, because it is quite rich, but oh so delicious.

Ingredients

2 Spanish onions, chopped
2 cloves garlic, minced
2 tablespoons olive oil

400g arborio rice
200ml full bodied red wine
3 tablespoons tomato paste
850ml rich beef, chicken or vegetable stock, simmering
4 fresh beetroots (about 600g)

1 tablespoon butter
2 tablespoons Parmesan cheese
freshly ground black pepper
½ bunch fresh chives
1 sweet potato
oil for frying

Method

Peel and trim all the beetroots and cut one of them into 1cm dice. Grate the remaining 3 beetroots.

Heat the oil and sauté the onions and garlic until softened. Add the rice and stir to coat. Add the red wine and mix well while the wine is being absorbed. When all the liquid is gone, add the tomato paste and the grated beetroot and the beetroot dice.

Begin adding the stock, half a cup at a time, stirring well after each addition and allowing each quantity to be absorbed before adding the next amount of stock.

When all the stock has been added and absorbed, remove the saucepan from the heat and stir in the butter, cheese, half the chopped chives and black pepper to taste.

Spoon into individual bowls and garnish with sweet potato chips and plenty of chopped chives.

Note

To make the sweet potato chips, peel and cut the sweet potatoes into very thin slices, sprinkling with salt. Heat some oil in a saucepan until smoking (about 180°C), add the potato slices and allow them to cook until crisp—about 3 minutes. (If the potato slices do not sizzle immediately when placed in the oil, remove and raise the temperature of the oil, then cook the sweet potato slices. It is very important that the oil be hot so that the chips are not greasy.)

Spanish Risotto

I had a wonderful time experimenting with ideas and recipes while researching this book. I found no reason why accepted flavour combinations could not work with risotto; in fact, many of these combinations were enhanced by the initial sautéing and subsequent slow cooking necessary to perfect risotto. This is one recipe that exemplifies this theory. The rice is full of flavour and colour and makes a perfect light lunch dish. The secret ingredient is the zest and juice of an orange. The citrus flavour is not distinguishable in the finished dish, yet when omitted, the risotto does not sparkle with flavour.

Ingredients

2 tablespoons olive oil
2 tablespoons mild paprika
¼ teaspoon chilli flakes or ½ teaspoon fresh chilli
1 teaspoon turmeric
good pinch of saffron threads
2 onions, sliced thinly
4 cloves garlic, minced
2 skinless boneless chicken breasts, sliced thinly
zest and juice of 1 orange

400g arborio rice
180ml white wine
900ml rich vegetable, chicken or beef stock, simmering
2 tablespoons tomato paste
½ cup parsley, chopped

4 spring onions, very finely chopped
extra fresh herbs
freshly ground black pepper

Method

Add the saffron threads to the hot stock and allow to rest.

Heat the olive oil in a large saucepan and add the paprika, chilli, turmeric and garlic. Cook for 1 minute to release the aroma of the spices. Add the onions and chicken and cook until onions are very soft and the chicken is opaque.

Add the rice and stir to coat, followed by the wine. Stir frequently while the wine is being absorbed. When all the liquid has disappeared, add the tomato paste, parsley and orange juice and zest. Continue cooking and stirring, adding the stock, half a cup at a time, stirring well after each addition. Continue in this manner until all the stock has been absorbed and the rice is firm but tender. Remove the saucepan from the heat, add the finely sliced spring onions, plenty of fresh herbs and black pepper and, serve immediately

Variation:

If preferred, cook the chicken breasts separately, slice on the diagonal and fan out over the risotto.

Australian Flavours

There is no doubt that Australia is indeed 'The Lucky Country'!

We have such a wide range of superb produce from which to select our ingredients, and the average consumer is becoming more aware of quality, enabling us to limit the amount of inferior imported ingredients available for purchase.

Our fruit and vegetable produce is among the finest in the world, and with the arrival of various migrant groups from Asia, the Australian diet is beginning to incorporate such exotica as bok choy and tatsoi as normal vegetable choices.

Tasmanian salmon has long been recognised as one of our greatest exports and its quality is unsurpassed. Yabbies have been an Aussie favourite for generations and feature in this chapter. Our lamb, poultry and beef are also of a high quality and feature strongly in the Australian diet.

Now, with an increasing interest in 'bush tucker' we are becoming more familiar with indigenous fruits and vegetables such as the Quandong, Kakadu plum and Bunya Bunya nut. There is also a strong trend toward an interest in 'new' meats such as crocodile, kangaroo, emu and buffalo.

With the amazing cultural diversity in Australia, our national cuisine is constantly changing to meet the demands and expectations of our new citizens. Born and bred Australians are also adopting many previously foreign tastes and these will constantly change what is perceived to be truly Australian.

Suffice it to say that with the traditional Australian flavours, the diverse mixture of ethnic tastes and the indigenous influence, our wonderful Australian cuisine is ever changing and evolving.

Surf and Turf Risotto

How well I remember feeling oh so sophisticated when I was in my mid-teens and dining with my parents in elegant restaurants. The dish of the day then was aptly named 'Surf and Turf' and always consisted of a beautiful piece of prime beef (usually sacrificed) with an elegantly curled lobster tail sitting precariously on top. This risotto is dedicated to that ubiquitous memory, and if I do say so myself, this recipe is quite delicious!

Ingredients

2 tablespoons olive oil
2 x 200g pieces of eye fillet
4 cloves garlic
10 spring onions, chopped
1 red capsicum, sliced into strips

400g arborio rice
150ml dry white wine
900ml rich vegetable or chicken stock, simmering
2 lobster tails, cooked
20 fresh basil leaves

1 tablespoon Parmesan cheese, grated
1 tablespoon sour cream
lots of fresh parsley, chopped

2 onions, peeled and sliced
oil for frying

Method

Heat the olive oil and gently fry the garlic for a moment or two. Add the beef and sauté until seared and crisp on both sides. Remove from the pan and keep warm wrapped in foil (for medium or well-done beef, bake at 200°C for 5 minutes or 10 minutes respectively, then keep warm wrapped in foil).

To the oil/garlic mixture, add the spring onions and capsicum strips and sauté until softened.

Add the rice and stir to coat, then add the wine and simmer to evaporate the alcohol while the liquid is absorbed. When the rice mixture is firm, add the stock, half a cup at a time, stirring well after each addition and allowing each quantity of stock to be absorbed before the next addition. Continue in this fashion until the stock has all been incorporated. With the last addition of stock, add the basil leaves and lobster meat, cut into attractive, manageable pieces, and stir to distribute.

Peel and slice the onions. Either deep fry at 180°C until crisp and golden, or alternatively, toss with 2 tablespoons olive oil and bake at 220°C for 30-40 minutes, tossing frequently, until golden. Set aside until the risotto is finished and ready to serve.

When almost all of the liquid has been absorbed and the rice is 'al dente', stir through the Parmesan cheese, parsley and sour cream.

Meanwhile, remove the warm meat from the foil and slice thinly.

Serve the risotto in individual bowls, fan out the meat and place on top of the risotto. Garnish with the crispy fried (or baked) onions and serve immediately.

Tomato and Tuna Risotto

(photographed on page 43)

Although the name of this risotto is not particularly inspirational, the results are stunning. A rich, flavourful risotto will reward your efforts here. You will be able to prepare this dish with no warning at all. Most of the produce will live on your pantry shelf, with only normal kitchen staples needed.

Ingredients

2 tablespoons olive oil
2 tablespoons fresh rosemary spikes
$\frac{1}{4}$ teaspoon chilli flakes or $\frac{1}{2}$ teaspoon fresh chilli
2 onions, sliced thinly
4 cloves garlic, crushed

400g arborio rice
180ml white wine
900ml rich vegetable stock, simmering
400g can Sirena Tuna, flaked
2 tablespoons La Gina Tomato Paste
2 tablespoons La Gina sun-dried tomatoes, chopped
400g can La Gina Italian tomatoes
$\frac{1}{2}$ cup parsley, chopped

4 spring onions, very finely chopped
4 tablespoons sour cream or mascarpone cheese
2 fresh roma tomatoes
extra fresh herbs
freshly ground black pepper

Method

In a sauté pan, heat the olive oil and add the rosemary spikes, chilli, garlic and onion. Cook over a high heat until the vegetables are soft and the aroma of the chilli and rosemary is noticeable.

Add the arborio rice and stir well to coat each grain of rice in the oil. Add the wine and simmer over high heat until the liquid has been absorbed and the alcoholic aroma has disappeared.

With the first addition of stock, add the flaked tuna, tomato paste, sun-dried tomatoes, canned tomatoes and parsley, and continue to stir and simmer until all liquid has been absorbed.

Continue adding stock ladle by ladle, allowing each to be absorbed before adding the next addition.

Once you have added the last addition of stock, remove the pan from the heat and add half the sour cream.

Garnish with a small dollop of remaining sour cream, finely diced fresh tomatoes and chopped spring onions. Add a sprinkle of extra fresh herbs if you like, and some black pepper.

Lamb and Rosella Flower Risotto

The delightfully different flavours in this risotto make a perfect summer dinner. The bright pink flowers take their name from their similarity in appearance to the bird of the same name. A simple but delicious accompaniment of a mixed lettuce salad dressed with raspberry vinaigrette would complete the picture. The rosella flowers taste a little like rhubarb and I have successfully substituted both rhubarb and sour cherries when rosella flowers were unavailable.

Ingredients

2 tablespoons macadamia nut oil
2 leeks, sliced and well washed
6 lamb backstrap fillets (about 700g), cut into slices
250g rosella flowers, frozen
2 teaspoons cinnamon
1 small red chilli, minced

400g arborio rice
100ml white wine
900ml light vegetable or chicken stock, simmering

200g baby spinach
100ml sour cream
rind and juice of 1 lemon
½ cup toasted macadamia nuts, lightly crushed
salt and pepper to taste

Method

In a saucepan, heat the macadamia oil and sauté the leeks until shiny and soft. Add the lamb slices, chilli and the cinnamon and stir well to combine. Add the rosella flowers and cook until the lamb changes colour and a pungent aroma of spice wafts from the pan.

Add the rice and stir to coat, then add the wine and simmer until all the liquid has been absorbed.

Begin adding the stock, 1 cup at a time, remembering to allow each addition to be absorbed before adding the next quantity of stock.

When all the liquid has been incorporated, add the spinach, sour cream, zest and juice of a lemon and salt and pepper to taste, and stir well.

Garnish with crushed macadamia nuts and serve immediately.

Variation

Can be served with lamb pieces over risotto and garnished with macadamia nuts.

Risotto of Gingered Barramundi with Bok Choy

The firm, sweet texture of barramundi is delicious when cooked this way. The ginger helps to bring out the sweetness of the fish and bok choy is a perfect addition, emphasising the Asian influence. The finely chopped garnish of coriander and mango provides a light, sweet tang, as well as another element of flavours—a perfect summer dish!

Ingredients

30g butter
700g barramundi fillets

1 tablespoon olive oil
2 white onions, chopped
2 cloves garlic, crushed
2 teaspoons minced fresh ginger

400g arborio rice
200ml white wine
800ml fish or vegetable stock, simmering
6 baby bok choy, cut into quarters

juice of 1 lime
½ bunch coriander
1 large firm mango
1 red chilli, finely chopped
salt and pepper to taste

Method

Heat the butter and quickly sear the barramundi on both sides until golden and crisp, set aside. Heat the olive oil and add the onions, garlic and ginger. Sauté for 5 minutes until softened and aromatic. Add the rice and stir to coat, then add the wine. Allow the liquid to be absorbed by the rice while the alcohol is evaporated.

Begin adding the stock, half a cup at a time, stirring thoroughly after each addition. Always allow each previously added quantity of stock to be absorbed before the next addition.

With the second addition of stock, add the bok choy and stir to distribute. Continue adding stock in the usual fashion until the rice is 'al dente'. With the last addition of stock, add the cubed barramundi and stir gently to combine. Season to taste with salt and pepper.

Meanwhile, in a separate bowl, mix together the chopped fresh coriander, lime juice, chilli and peeled and finely diced mango.

To serve, mound the risotto in individual platters and top with a generous quantity of mango coriander salsa.

Risotto of Venison, Juniper Berries and Red Cabbage

This rich and appealing risotto is full of Australian flavours. The venison is very low in fat, so remember to sauté it just until the colour changes. The addition of the berries and red cabbage provides a little sweetness and rich flavours, fully enhanced by the apples.

Ingredients

2 tablespoons olive oil
8 shallots, chopped
600g venison, either rump or saddle cut, preferably farmed venison
400g arborio rice
120ml red wine
900ml rich beef, veal or vegetable stock, simmering
1/2 small red cabbage
1/4 cup juniper berries
2 Granny Smith apples
4 tablespoons extra stock
1 tablespoon butter
1/3 cup Italian parsley, chopped

Method

Heat the olive oil and sauté the shallots until slightly golden. Raise the heat and cook the venison quickly until the colour changes.

Reduce the heat to medium, add the rice and stir to coat. Add the red wine and allow the alcohol to evaporate while the liquid is absorbed. Add the first addition of stock, stirring thoroughly to distribute. With the second addition of stock, add the finely sliced cabbage, juniper berries and peeled and diced Granny Smith apples. Stir to combine.

Continue adding stock in the usual manner until the liquid has almost all been absorbed, and the rice is tender but still a little firm.

Add the extra hot stock, butter and herbs, stir vigorously and serve.

Risotto of Kangaroo and Kakadu Plum

This rich, satisfying risotto makes a perfect main course. Chicken will work equally well if you find the thought of eating kangaroo offensive, but once you try this combination, I think you will be able to forget the relationship to 'Skippy'.

Ingredients

2 tablespoons olive oil
2 leeks, well washed and sliced
650g kangaroo fillets, cut into strips

400g arborio rice
50ml port or sherry
50ml white wine
900ml vegetable or chicken stock, simmering
300g snow or sugar peas
1 pack frozen Kakadu plums
2 tablespoons tomato paste
zest of 1 orange

10 slices kangaroo prosciutto
1 leek
oil for frying

Method

Heat the olive oil and sauté the cleaned leeks until softened and translucent. Add the kangaroo fillet strips and stir to cook gently.

Add the arborio rice and stir to coat. Add the port and white wine and simmer until the liquid has all been absorbed. Add the tomato paste and mix thoroughly. Begin adding the vegetable stock, half a cup at a time, and stir well after each addition. When half the stock has been absorbed, add the Kakadu plums. Continue adding stock and stirring as above until the last addition.

Meanwhile, prepare the garnish. Wash the extra leek very well, then cut into long thin strips. Heat oil to a temperature of 180°C and deep fry the leeks until golden. Using tongs, bunch up the leeks as you remove them from the oil and drain on absorbent paper. To crisp the prosciutto, lay between two sheets of paper towel and microwave on 'high' for 30 seconds. To test, allow to cool then see if the prosciutto is brittle. If not, microwave until the desired crispness is achieved.

With the last addition of stock, add the snow peas and zest of orange, and season to taste with salt and pepper.

Serve in individual bowls, garnished with a tangle of deep fried leeks and some crisp prosciutto.

Risotto of Marinated Buffalo and Fresh Asparagus

Buffalo is farmed mostly in the Northern Territory then exported overseas. As time goes by it will become more commonly available, and although somewhat 'gamey', it is similar to beef. Marinating the meat allows the flavours to become more refined.

Ingredients

800g buffalo, thinly sliced
250ml red wine
50ml soy sauce
2 tablespoons mild mustard

2 tablespoons peanut oil
1 brown onion, chopped
½ bunch fresh chives, chopped

400g arborio rice
marinating liquid
2 tablespoons tomato paste
800ml rich beef stock, simmering
500g sweet potatoes, peeled and thinly sliced (¼ sweet potato reserved for garnish)
500g fresh asparagus
½ bunch fresh basil, chopped
salt and pepper to taste

Method

The day before you make your risotto, mix together the marinating ingredients and pour over the meat in a non-reactive bowl or platter. Allow the meat to marinate for at least 12 hours, preferably 24 hours.

On the day, heat the peanut oil and sauté the onion and chives until softened. Remove the buffalo from the marinade. Add to the onion mixture and cook until the meat changes colour.

Add the rice and stir to coat, then add the marinating mixture. Simmer until the liquid has been absorbed, stirring well to avoid the rice sticking to the pot. Add the sliced sweet potato and tomato paste and stir thoroughly to combine. Begin adding stock, half a cup at a time, stirring well after each addition.

Meanwhile, heat a little extra oil and deep fry the remaining piece of sweet potato that has been sliced with a vegetable peeler into fine slices. When golden and crisp, drain on absorbent paper.

With the last addition of stock, add the fresh asparagus, cut into diagonal pieces about 3cm long, and the basil, and combine gently. Season to taste with salt and pepper and serve with crisp sweet potato chips.

Risotto of Chilli-spiked Yabby with Ginger

Yabbies are as much a part of Australian life as Vegemite. Most little boys would remember taking a container down to a stream or pond during their childhood, searching for frogs and tadpoles, only to be rewarded with a brown spiny creature. These days, yabbies are commonplace on restaurant menus and have a delicious sweet flavour. You can buy yabbies from fish and shellfish suppliers already cooked, but if you are lucky enough to have your own source, simply soak overnight in salty water then boil in fresh water until brightly coloured. Cool then peel, save the claws for garnish if desired, but use the meat from the tails.

Ingredients

2 tablespoons peanut oil
1 brown onion, chopped
3 small, fresh red chillies, minced
4cm piece of fresh ginger or 2 teaspoons ground ginger
20 cooked yabbies, peeled

400g arborio rice
100ml white wine
900ml fish stock (or vegetable), simmering
4 firm tomatoes, roughly chopped
3 shallots, sliced

2 tablespoons cream
fresh sage leaves, fried until crisp
salt and pepper to taste

Method

Heat the peanut oil and add the onion, chilli and ginger, sautéing for a moment or two until the onion has softened. Add the yabby meat and toss in the onion/chilli mixture to coat. With a slotted spoon, remove the yabbies and keep warm.

To the onion/chilli mixture, add the rice and stir to coat. Add the white wine and allow the alcohol to be evaporated while the liquid is absorbed. Begin adding fish stock, half a cup at a time, allowing each addition to be well absorbed before adding the next addition. Stir well, often, to encourage the separation of starch from the rice. When half the liquid has been absorbed, add the chopped tomatoes and shallots, continuing adding stock as necessary.

When all the liquid has been added and the rice is still slightly firm, add the cream and salt and pepper to taste.

Stir thoroughly and serve, garnished with crisp sage leaves.

Smoked Trout and Goat's Cheese Risotto

This risotto is one of my favourites. It is full of rich, elegant flavours from ingredients that are easy to purchase and require no prior cooking. Lots of fresh herbs help to lighten this lovely dish.

Ingredients

1 Spanish onion, sliced
2 cloves garlic, crushed
½ cup parsley, chopped
2 tablespoons olive oil

400g arborio rice
100ml white wine
900ml vegetable stock, simmering
200g Warrigal spinach (or traditional English spinach if unavailable)
3 fillets smoked trout
150g Australian goat's cheese

2 tablespoons sour cream or yoghurt
½ cup fresh dill
½ cup fresh basil
½ cup fresh coriander, plus extra sprigs for garnish
salt and freshly ground pepper

Method

Heat the olive oil and sauté the onion, garlic and parsley until the vegetables have softened.

Add the rice and stir to coat. Add the wine and allow the alcohol to evaporate while the liquid is being absorbed. Add the first quantity of hot stock and stir well while the rice simmers. As each quantity of stock is absorbed, add another half cup, stirring again. Continue in this manner until half the stock has been incorporated.

Add the well-washed Warrigal spinach and stir to combine. Continue adding stock as above.

With the last addition of stock, add the flaked trout, goat's cheese, sour cream (or yoghurt) and all the fresh herbs. Combine gently while the last of the liquid is absorbed. As soon as the rice is firm but tender, serve in individual bowls garnished with a sprig or two of coriander.

Asian Risotto Flavours

When *beginning this chapter, I really had to put my 'classical' ideas behind me and allow the flavours I adore from countries like Thailand, Malaysia, India and China to shine through. Although the recipes that follow are in no way traditional or classical, nor are they faddish or trendy.*

The *flavour combinations have been around in one form or another, in the aforementioned countries, for centuries, paired with rice or noodle dishes that are specific to that region.*

I *have always known that rice cooked in the simple, specific way of risotto creates a wonderful vehicle to showcase a multitude of flavours. The risotto way of cooking produces very different flavours and textures that would never taste the same when prepared as fried rice, for example, or a pilaf.*

I *implore you to try these unusual yet delicious combinations, and I'm sure that you will agree that these recipes only add to your repertoire.*

Salads
the art of creating cool food

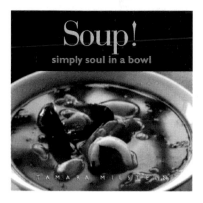

Soup!
simply soul in a bowl

risotto 'round the world!

CONVERSIONS

stuff it!
the art of creating filled food

Risotto
'round the world!

bake your cake & eat it too!

Bread

To be released March 2000

Measurements

All cup and spoon measurements are level.

Australian		USA Equivalent	
tsp	5ml	tsp	$1/6$ oz
tbspn	20ml	tbspn	$2/3$ oz
cup	250ml	cup	8 oz
	30g		1 oz
	50g		$1 2/3$ oz
	200g		7 oz
	250g		8 oz
	400g		14 oz
	500g		16 oz
	600g		21 oz
	700g		25 oz
	800g		28 oz
	1kg		35 oz
	100ml		$3 1/2$ fl oz
	120ml		4 fl oz
	150ml		5 fl oz
	300ml		10 fl oz
	400ml		$13 1/2$ fl oz
	500ml		$16 1/2$ fl oz
	700ml		$23 1/2$ fl oz
	800ml		$26 1/2$ fl oz
	900ml		1 qt
	1l		33 fl oz

Temperatures

160°C	320°F	190°C	370°F
170°C	330°F	200°C	390°F
180°C	350°F	250°C	480°F

Convenient tear-out bookmark

GLOSSARY

barramundi fillets	firm textured, white fish filllets
beetroot	regular round beet
blue eye cod	cod fish
butternut pumpkin	butternut squash
capsicum	bell pepper
chickpeas	garbanzos
coriander	cilantro
green peas	snap peas
Kakadu plums	native Australian plum
lamb backstrap fillets	lean lamb fillets
lemon zest	lemon rind
minced	ground
prawns	shrimp
prunes	whole dried plums
pumpkin seeds	pepita
punnet	small basket ~ 8 oz
roma tomatoes	sauce tomatoes
rosella flowers	native Australian flower
shallots	French eschallots
skirt steak	flank steak
snapper	red snapper
snow peas	mange tout
spring onions	scallions
sultanas	seedless white raisins
yabbies	fresh water crayfish

Length (approx.)

1cm	1/3"	5cm	2"
2cm	3/4"	15cm	6"
2.5cm	1"	40cm	16"

If you have enjoyed the innovation, variety and delicious flavours of any one of Tamara's fantastic cookbooks, you should try others in the series—you most certainly will not be disappointed. Listed below is a brief synopsis of each of her books.

Bake Your Cake and Eat It Too *presents a mouthwatering variety of cakes, both sweet and savoury. Tamara's easy-to-follow recipes will have you baking up a storm, creating cakes that will soon become family favourites. From the Asian-influenced* Chinese Ginger Syrup Cake *to the savoury* Eggplant and Goat Cheese Cake, *there is a recipe to suit any occasion, to follow any meal or to satisfy the most discerning tastebud.*

Stuff It! the art of creating filled food: *why not try your hand at the art of creating filled food with Tamara's fantastic book. Filled Italian pasta, Mexican street foods, Asian rice paper rolls and Indian samosas—create a startling array of marvellous finger foods which tantalise the tastebuds.*

Risotto 'round the world *features modern-flavoured risottos which incorporate taste-tantalising ingredients in wonderful recipes from all four corners of the earth. While they remain true to the traditional method of making risotto, they allow the flavours of exotic ingredients to share the limelight.*

Soup! simply soul in a bowl: *this wonderfully versatile cookbook features hearty soups to nourish and satisfy, as well as light and refreshing soups which can be served either hot or chilled. Complete with a range of low-fat soups, which don't taste low-fat at all.*

Salads! the art of creating cool food: *in this book Tamara has created a beautiful range of salads from around the world. From Australia to Zambia, you can experience the best the world has to offer. Try* Couscous Salad with Seafood and Fresh Mint *or* Warm Mediterranean Salsa of Eggplant, Tomato and Roasted Garlic *or, for the more traditional, the best Caesar salad you will ever try.*

Breads! *Tamara's original cooking classes were based on bread cooking. We now find that more and more home cooks are baking their own bread, some using new electric bread makers whilst others are prepared to bake by the traditional method. This book covers all areas, with some of the best-tasting breads you will ever bake. From flat breads to sweet breads, you will have a great deal of enjoyment using the tried and true recipes Tamara has included in this book.*

If you have any difficulty in obtaining a copy of any of the above titles, just contact the publisher at the address below: R&R Publications Marketing Pty Ltd, PO Box 254, Carlton North, Victoria 3054, Australia.

Telephone (03) 9381 2199 Fax (03) 9381 2689, or call our National Toll-free number: 1 800 063 296. E-mail:richardc@bigpond.net.au

Risotto of Madras Tuna

What an unusual recipe this is! An ethnic mix of Indian spices, Pacific fish and Italian cooking styles have all combined to create this low fat, high flavour dish. I like to serve it as a main course, simply because I can never decide what to serve after it that will still complement the flavours. An Asian-style salad of lime-dressed vegetables would be a perfect accompaniment.

Ingredients

2 tablespoons butter
1 carrot, finely chopped
1 stick celery, finely chopped
1 onion, finely chopped
½ cup parsley, finely chopped
300g fresh tuna steaks
1 litre vegetable stock
pinch of saffron threads

1 tablespoon olive oil
2 teaspoons Madras curry powder
2 teaspoons turmeric
1 onion, finely chopped

400g arborio rice
150ml white wine
6 roma tomatoes

2 tablespoons yoghurt
½ cup fresh parsley, chopped

Method

First, poach the fish. In a saucepan, melt the butter and sauté the carrot, celery, onion and parsley until the vegetables are softened. Add the vegetable stock and simmer for 5 minutes. Add the fish and ground saffron threads and simmer for 10-15 minutes, or until the fish flakes easily when tested. Remove the fish from the stock and cut into 1cm cubes. Reserve the stock for the risotto.

Heat the olive oil and sauté the chopped onion, curry powder and turmeric. Add the rice and stir to coat. Add the wine and stir until the wine has been absorbed. Next add the chopped tomatoes, followed by half a cup of stock. Stir well to incorporate.

Continue adding half a cup of stock at a time, and allow each addition to be absorbed before adding the next quantity of stock. When adding the last addition of stock, add the tuna and stir gently to combine. Remove the pan from the heat, add yoghurt if desired, or serve with yoghurt and parsley on top of each serve as a garnish. Serve immediately.

Risotto of Indian Spiced Chicken with Chickpeas

(photographed on page 61)

The aromatic spices that marinate the chicken in this dish create delicious, musky sweet flavours that permeate the rice. The chicken will benefit from a long marination of at least 6 hours, but if time is scarce, an hour or two will do. I like to serve this risotto with a simple raita, a yoghurt-based sauce flavoured with cucumber, lemon juice and herbs. You will notice that I have omitted the wine in this recipe, simply because there are so many flavours that I find it superfluous. If you would like to add wine, simply add 200ml after toasting the rice, and remember to reduce your stock by the same amount.

Ingredients

4 boneless, skinless thigh fillets cut into strips, or
12 'winglets'
3 cloves garlic, crushed
2 teaspoons ground cumin
2 teaspoons paprika
2 teaspoons ground coriander
1 tablespoon garam masala
1 teaspoon ground ginger
3 tablespoons mango or apricot chutney
juice and zest of 1 orange
4 tablespoons olive oil

1 tablespoon ghee
1 bunch spring onions, trimmed and chopped
400g arborio rice
1 litre well flavoured vegetable stock
400g can chickpeas, drained and rinsed
2 handfuls baby spinach, washed
100g sultanas

2 tablespoons yoghurt, optional
2 tablespoons fresh mint, chopped
salt and freshly ground pepper to taste
100g toasted almonds

Method

In a glass jug, mix together the garlic, cumin, paprika, coriander, garam masala, ginger, chutney, orange juice and zest, and oil. Mix very well then pour over the chicken in a non-reactive baking dish (glass or ceramic) and allow to marinate for 6 hours of overnight.

In a saucepan, heat the ghee and add half the spring onions and cook gently until softened. Remove the chicken from the marinade and add to the spring onions, cooking until the chicken begins to change colour, about 3 minutes.

Remove chicken from pan, add rice and begin adding the stock, half a cup at a time and allowing each to be absorbed before the next quantity of stock is added. When adding the last of the stock, add the chickpeas, baby spinach and sultanas and mix vigorously to incorporate. When the liquid has been absorbed, remove the saucepan from the heat and add the cooked chicken, spring onions, yoghurt, fresh mint and salt and pepper to taste.

Serve immediately, garnished with the toasted almonds.

Note

For a more intense flavour, add as much of the marinade as you like to the saucepan at the same time as adding the chicken.

Persian Risotto

This lovely recipe has all the components of true ethnicity. Persia is at the crossroads of both Asia and the Middle East and therefore borrows flavours from both. I love serving this dish because it has so many layers of flavour and texture, and each mouthful seems more delicious than the last. I have specified lamb, but chicken or beef work just as well.

Ingredients

3 tablespoons olive oil
2 teaspoons cumin
2 cinnamon sticks
6 cloves garlic, minced
2 large brown onions, roughly chopped
600g lamb fillets, sliced
200g walnuts, toasted and cut in half

400g arborio rice
$\frac{1}{3}$ cup pomegranate juice or molasses (available at Middle Eastern stores)
1 litre vegetable stock, simmering

5 fresh dates, chopped
100g dried apricots, whole
10 prunes, whole

2 tablespoons mild yoghurt
100g toasted pistachio nuts, roughly chopped
1 cup fresh coriander or basil, to serve

Method

In a large saucepan, add the oil, cumin, garlic and cinnamon sticks, and cook for 1 minute. Add the lamb and cook over a high heat, stirring constantly until the lamb changes colour, about 3 minutes. Add the brown onions and continue cooking until the onions soften, about 3 minutes. Add the ground walnuts and stir vigorously to combine.

Add the rice and stir to coat. Add the pomegranate juice or molasses and mix thoroughly. Begin adding stock, half a cup at a time, stirring well after each addition and allowing each quantity to be absorbed before the next stock is added.

Halfway through the cooking time, add the dates, prunes and apricots and continue adding stock in the usual manner.

When all the stock has been added, remove the pan from the heat and add the yoghurt and half the coriander. Serve in individual bowls and garnish with remaining coriander and toasted pistachio nuts.

Asian Mushroom and Sesame Risotto

The flavour of Chinese mushrooms is spectacular—smoky, musky and very flavoursome. I have suggested a mixture of dried and fresh mushrooms which gives the best texture, but if you cannot find one or the other, just use more of the mushrooms that are available.

Ingredients

1 tablespoon olive oil
1 tablespoon sesame oil
2 brown onions, sliced
1 clove garlic, minced
3 tablespoon sesame seeds

15g black cloud fungus*
15g dried shiitake mushrooms*
150g fresh oyster mushrooms*
400g arborio rice
100ml Chinese rice wine
900ml vegetable stock, simmering
100g canned abalone mushrooms*
100g canned bean shoots

20 Thai basil leaves
2 tablespoons soy sauce, or to taste
additional sesame seeds for sprinkling

available from Asian food stores

Method

Soak the black cloud fungus and shiitake mushrooms in boiling hot water for 30 minutes.

Heat the oils and add the sliced brown onions, garlic and sesame seeds. Sauté until the seeds are deep golden and the onions are softened.

Add the rice and stir to coat. Add the rice wine and stir while allowing the liquid to absorb. Add the first half cup of stock, together with the soaked and drained mushrooms. Stir well to combine. Continue adding half a cup of stock at a time, stirring well after each addition. When adding the remaining half a cup of stock, add the abalone mushrooms and bean shoots and cook for 2 minutes more.

Remove the pan from the heat and add the torn basil leaves and soy sauce to taste. Serve immediately, sprinkled with additional sesame seeds.

Thai Chilli Tuna Risotto

The beauty of this dish is in the convenience of this wonderful new tuna product. Sirena Chilli Tuna is full of flavour, and if you have a can or two in your pantry you will never be caught short. I have emphasised the Asian flavours in this dish by adding typical Thai flavours such as coriander and a little fish sauce. If you prefer, of course, you can leave them out.

Ingredients

2 tablespoons peanut oil
½ cup fresh coriander, chopped
2 tablespoons lime juice
2 tablespoons fish sauce
½ bunch spring onions
250g button mushrooms

400g arborio rice
150ml white wine
1 litre vegetable or fish stock
200g oyster mushrooms
400g can Sirena Chilli Tuna
1 handful of baby spinach or 4 silverbeet leaves, trimmed and well washed

50g Chinese rice stick (dried noodles shaped into a bundle)
½ cup fresh coriander, chopped
16 large basil leaves, fried until crisp, to garnish

Method

Heat the peanut oil and sauté the spring onions briefly. Add the sliced button mushrooms and sauté. Add the coriander, fish sauce and lime juice and cook for 2 more minutes, until most of the liquid has evaporated.

Add the rice and stir to coat. Add the white wine and allow the liquid to absorb while stirring. Begin adding stock, half a cup at a time, stirring well after each addition. When half the liquid has been absorbed, add the tuna and oyster mushrooms and stir well. Continue adding stock as usual. When adding the last quantity of stock, add the spinach and stir well. Remove the pan from the heat.

To prepare the noodles, simply crush with your hands and drop into hot oil. Allow to sizzle until golden, about 30 seconds (you may like to do them in several small batches).

Serve the risotto in individual bowls, garnished with deep fried crispy noodles, coriander and crisp basil leaves.

Note

When deep frying basil, be aware it will spit badly, it may be prudent to place a mesh strainer over the top of the deep fryer for a few seconds.

Peking Duck Risotto

This very elegant and delightful risotto is based on one that I first tried in San Francisco. I was delighted by the flavours and textures of this San Franciscan version, and while testing with ordinary roast duck I found the flavours were nowhere near as spectacular. I haven't given instructions for making the Peking Duck from scratch because it is an involved and time consuming process. I find it much simpler to purchase one from a reputable Chinese food store or butcher in Chinatown. Save this recipe for when you really want to impress a special friend.

Ingredients

1 tablespoon olive oil
1 tablespoon toasted sesame oil
8 spring onions, finely chopped

400g arborio rice
200ml dry white wine
800ml rich duck stock (see note)
1 cooked Peking Duck
4 baby bok choy halved or quartered lengthways
200g sliced water chestnuts, drained

½ cup boiling duck stock, extra
3 tablespoons fresh coriander, chopped
3 tablespoons fresh parsley, chopped
spring onion greens to garnish
salt and pepper to taste

Method

If the Peking duck is whole, cut it into manageable portions and strip all the flesh from the bones, and reserve skin. Slice and set aside until required.

In a saucepan, heat the olive and sesame oils and add the spring onions. Cook gently for two minutes until softened, then add the rice and stir to coat. Add the wine and allow the liquid to absorb while stirring. Begin adding the stock, half a cup at a time, stirring very well after each addition and always allowing each previous quantity of stock to be absorbed before adding the next amount. With the second addition of stock, add the bok choy. When half the stock has been used, add the Peking duck and stir to incorporate. Continue adding stock in the usual manner.

With the last addition of stock, add the drained water chestnuts. When all the liquid has been absorbed, remove the pan from the heat. Add all the remaining fresh herbs and mix well. Serve the risotto garnished with crispy duck skin.

Variation

Risotto can be in individual bowls and make a small well in the centre of each. Pour a tablespoon of boiling duck stock into each indentation and serve immediately with spring onion curls (see below).

Note

To make duck stock, take 1.5 litres of chicken stock and add the duck frame and all off-cuts and bones (from the Peking duck) and bring to the boil. Add two bay leaves and some peppercorns and simmer for 30 minutes. Taste and season if necessary. If the flavour is not strong enough, simmer for a further 15 minutes. Strain, discarding all duck pieces and reserving stock. When measured, you should have just over 1 litre.

To make spring onion curls, cut the long green ends of the spring onion to lengths of about 15cm. With a sharp knife, make long cuts through the onion strips, but leaving 1cm uncut at one end. Plunge these into icy cold water for 2 hours or longer, until curled. Drain and garnish the risotto.

Risotto of Chinese Aromatics

Your guests will be able to smell the fragrances of this risotto long before it reaches the table. The pungent aromas help create a delicious and quite unusual dining experience that will leave you asking for more. Serve with some lightly stir-fried Chinese vegetables or a light fish dish.

Ingredients

15g black cloud fungus (or Chinese dried mushrooms)
1 cup boiling water to soak

1 tablespoon olive oil
1 tablespoon toasted sesame oil
1 bunch spring onions
2 cloves garlic, minced
1-2 tablespoons grated fresh ginger
½ teaspoon fresh chopped red chillies

400g arborio rice
200ml light dry white wine
1 tablespoon fish sauce
2 tablespoons soy sauce, or to taste
1 tablespoon Chinese black bean sauce
½ cup fresh mint, chopped
½ cup fresh coriander, chopped
800ml vegetable stock, simmering
½ cup bean shoots

2 tablespoon fresh coriander
150g piece tofu, cut into dice
2 teaspoons toasted sesame oil, extra

Method

Soak the tree cloud fungus (or dried mushrooms) in boiling hot water for 30 minutes, then drain, saving the soaking liquid to add to the stock. Set aside the mushrooms.

In a saucepan, add the oils and spring onions, garlic, ginger and red chilli. Sauté for 3 minutes until the ginger releases its pungent aroma. Add the rice and stir to coat. Add the wine, soy sauce, fish sauce, black bean sauce and soaked mushrooms and allow absorption. Stir well to distribute the flavours. Strain the mushroom soaking liquid through a piece of muslin or paper towel to remove any sand or grit, and mix with the simmering stock. When the wine has all been absorbed, begin adding the stock, half a cup at a time. Continue adding stock, half a cup at time and stirring well after each addition. When adding the last quantity of stock, add the bean shoots and herbs.

When most of the stock has been absorbed, remove the pan from the heat, garnish with the tofu cubes, fresh coriander and a drizzle of sesame oil if desired. Serve immediately.

Malay Beef Risotto

Everyone is familiar with the flavours of satay. When creating this recipe I wanted the flavours of traditional Malay satay with a little extra bite. The chilli and lime juices serve this purpose wonderfully, and I have used regular peanut butter to make this recipe easy. You'll be surprised how mellow this dish is.

Ingredients

2 tablespoons sesame or peanut oil
500g lean beef, cubed
6 shallots, finely chopped
4 cloves garlic, minced
1 teaspoon cumin
½-1 teaspoon minced fresh red chilli

400g arborio rice
100ml rice wine
950ml beef stock (or vegetable), simmering
6 tablespoons chunky peanut butter
2 tablespoons soy sauce
400g Chinese cabbage, finely shredded

1 tablespoon lime juice
½ cup parsley, chopped
½ cup roasted peanuts, chopped

Method

Heat the sesame or peanut oil and add the shallots, garlic, cumin and chilli. Sauté for 2 minutes to release their flavour and aroma. Add the beef cubes and sauté well until they change colour—about 5 minutes.

Add the rice and stir to coat. Add the rice wine, stirring well until the liquid is absorbed. Add the peanut butter, soy sauce and half a cup of stock and stir well to incorporate flavours. When the liquid has been absorbed, add the next half cup of stock, together with the shredded Chinese cabbage. Continue cooking and stirring, adding half a cup of stock as necessary until almost all the liquid has been absorbed.

Remove the pan from the heat and serve in individual bowls, garnished with lime juice, chopped peanuts and parsley.

Variation

To make a vegetarian satay risotto, omit the beef. Cut 1 large carrot, 1 large parsnip and 1 large potato into large chunks, and add these to the risotto with 150g of cauliflower florets after the spices have been sautéed. Proceed as above.

Curried Squid and Coconut Risotto

The name of this recipe really does not do this dish justice. The richly-flavoured rice has mild curry overtones softened by the coconut milk, and the squid looks pretty and tastes delicious. It is important not to overcook the squid, otherwise it will be tough to eat.

Ingredients

2 tablespoons peanut oil
2 garlic cloves, minced
2 tablespoons ground coriander
1 teaspoon shrimp paste or 1 tablespoon fish sauce
grated rind of 1 lemon
½ teaspoon chilli powder
1-2 teaspoons curry powder
300g squid tube, cleaned (not calamari)
400g arborio rice
100ml rice wine
900ml vegetable or fish stock, simmering
1 cup thick coconut milk
1 can bamboo shoots, sliced
1 can water chestnuts, sliced
200g snow peas
3 tablespoons toasted coconut
3 tablespoons fresh coriander, chopped

Method

Heat the oil and sauté the garlic, coriander, fish sauce, lemon rind, chilli powder and curry powder until thick and fragrant. Meanwhile, cut the squid into manageable pieces and score the inside to create tiny 'diamond' shapes. Do not cut through to the outside.

Add the squid pieces to the spice mixture and sauté briefly until almost cooked, about 3 minutes.

Remove the squid and keep warm.

To the remaining spice mixture, add the rice and toast briefly. Add the rice wine and stir while the liquid is being absorbed. Begin adding the stock, half a cup at a time, stirring well after each addition and allowing the liquid to be absorbed before adding the next quantity of stock. When all the stock has been absorbed, add the coconut milk, water chestnuts, bamboo shoots, snow peas and coriander, simmer for 2 or 3 more minutes until most of the liquid has been absorbed.

Remove from heat and garnish with toasted coconut. Serve immediately.

Tex-Mex Flavours

I have enjoyed Mexican style food for many years. While travelling in the United States of America as a child I was encouraged to try new tastes and I remember washing down my first Mexican meal with litres of cold water. I didn't have the desire to eat Mexican again for several years. Anyway, living in Australia made it difficult to source the required ingredients to achieve a genuine result. When I travelled as an adult I found a wide range of flavours and textures attributable to the cuisine of Mexico. After a long and interesting culinary investigation into Mexican foods I have discovered that there is no need for the dishes of this region to be 'hotter than hot'. Of course, chilli plays an important part in the preparation of genuine Mexican foods, but handled correctly it can contribute amazing flavour with just the right amount of heat for your tastes.

'*T*ex-Mex' is the name of the more Western style Mexican cuisine that has evolved along the Mexico/Texas border and has become very popular across America. Use the flavours of traditional Mexican cuisine and adjust the seasoning to suit you. Since the world has become a much smaller place, we now have the luxury of worldwide food purveyors—you will find most of these more unusual ingredients in department store food halls and speciality shops.

Vegetarian Risotto Diablo

This risotto is full of intense, spicy flavours with a strong Mexican influence. Okra, chillies and red capsicums contribute smooth, hot and sweet flavours which all combine beautifully. The addition of finely diced fresh tomatoes on completion is an interesting technique which lightens and refreshes the flavours of the dish. A big pot of this risotto, some crusty bread and a green salad—a recipe for a perfect dinner!

Ingredients

2 onions, sliced
200g baby okra, washed and trimmed
2 tablespoons olive oil
1/2-1 teaspoon minced red chilli

400g arborio rice
100ml white wine
900ml vegetable stock
4 red capsicums, cut into chunks
2 x 400g tins red kidney beans

2 tablespoons stock, extra
2 roma tomatoes, finely chopped
10 sprigs coriander, chopped
100g sour cream (optional)

Method

Heat the olive oil and sauté the sliced onions and chilli together until the onions are softened. Add the okra and cook a further 2 minutes.

Add the rice and stir to coat, toasting the rice gently. Add the wine and stir while the liquid is absorbed. When the rice mixture is firm and dry, begin adding the stock, half a cup at a time, stirring well after each addition. With the second addition of stock, add all the capsicum chunks. When half the stock has been absorbed, add the drained and rinsed kidney beans. Continue adding stock and stirring well after each addition until all the stock has been absorbed.

When all the stock has been added, remove the pot from the heat and add the finely chopped fresh tomatoes and the extra stock, and stir thoroughly. Serve in individual bowls, garnished with a dollop of sour cream and plenty of coriander.

Nachos Risotto

(photographed on page 79)

What a contradiction in terms! Nachos of course refers to the delicious combination of toasted corn chips with a topping of refried beans, guacamole (mashed and flavoured avocado), mild or hot chilli sauce, green onions and sour cream. Although refried beans can be made from scratch, they are available in a can and are a high quality product. These flavours marry beautifully with risotto and I hope you enjoy this interesting experience.

Ingredients

2 ripe avocados, finely diced
1 small red capsicum, finely diced
1 small onion, finely minced
1 tablespoon lime juice
salt and pepper to taste

1 tablespoon corn oil (or olive oil)
$1/2$-1 teaspoon minced red chilli or $1/4$ teaspoon chilli flakes
1 Spanish onion, roughly chopped
6 spring onions, white part only and finely chopped, (greens reserved for garnish)

400g arborio rice
150ml white wine
800ml vegetable stock, simmering
1 x 400g can refried beans
200ml mild or hot taco sauce

To Garnish:
150ml sour cream
spring onion greens, finely sliced
reserved avocado salsa (see method)
70g corn chips

Method

First make the avocado salsa. In a bowl, add the avocado, minced onion, red capsicum, lime juice and salt and pepper to taste. Mix well and set aside.

Heat the corn or olive oil and add the chilli. Stir for one minute to release the aroma and pungency of the chilli, then add the Spanish onions and spring onions. Sauté until the onions are softened, and then add the rice and stir to coat.

Add the wine and allow the mixture to simmer while stirring until all the liquid has been absorbed. Begin adding the stock, half a cup at a time, stirring well as the liquid is absorbed. Continue adding stock this way until half the stock has been added. With the next addition of stock, add the refried beans and taco sauce, and stir thoroughly to combine. Continue stirring and adding stock until all the stock has been added.

Remove the saucepan from the heat and serve in individual bowls, garnished with sour cream, avocado salsa, green onions and corn chips.

Yucateco Seafood Risotto

This risotto combines so many interesting flavours, I find it hard to pick any one that stands out. The cream provides a silky smooth finish that is hard to beat. I find myself eating this one right down to the last grain of rice.

Ingredients

500g assorted seafood such as prawns, calamari and scallops
500g white fish fillets (no bones) such as blue eye
2 tablespoons olive oil
1/4-1/2 teaspoon minced chilli
2 cloves garlic

1 tablespoon olive oil
2 onions, sliced
400g arborio rice
200ml white wine
700ml rich fish stock, simmering
2 bay leaves
1/2 cup milk or hot taco sauce
2 ribs celery, sliced
2 large tomatoes, chopped
2 potatoes, peeled and diced
100ml cream

1 cup parsley, chopped
1 teaspoon paprika
2 potatoes, boiled and thinly sliced

Method

First prepare the shellfish. Cut the fish fillets into 2cm chunks and rinse the shellfish. Heat the olive oil and sauté the garlic, chilli and fish chunks until opaque. Remove with a slotted spoon and keep warm. Add the shellfish to the same pan and sauté until just cooked and changed colour, about 3 minutes. Remove the pan from the heat, return the fish and mix gently. Set aside.

In a large saucepan, heat the olive oil and sauté the onions. Add the rice and stir to coat, allowing the rice to become translucent. Add the wine and allow to simmer until the liquid evaporates. Add the bay leaves, potato cubes and celery with the first addition of half a cup of stock. Stir vigorously to combine. When the stock has been absorbed, add the next half cup of stock. Continue in this fashion, adding stock and stirring thoroughly until the last quantity of stock is to be added. At this time, add the chopped tomatoes, taco sauce, cream and half the parsley.

When all the ingredients have been added and most of the stock has been absorbed, remove the pan from the heat, remove the bay leaves and serve in individual bowls on a bed of boiled sliced potatoes, garnished with plenty of parsley and a sprinkling of paprika.

Risotto Mexicana

The inspiration for this recipe is a typical Mexican rice dish that is served stuffed into tomatoes and pumpkins. It has a much drier consistency than this version, which incorporates the traditional Italian style of making risotto, producing a creamier, more succulent texture. You will notice that I have chosen not to add wine to this risotto because it would totally change the flavour of this dish. If, however, you would like to add some wine after adding the rice, simply deduct that same quantity from the total quantity of the stock to adjust the liquid content.

Ingredients

1 teaspoon minced red chilli
2 cloves garlic, minced
2 onions, sliced
2 tablespoons olive oil

400g arborio rice
900ml rich vegetable stock, simmering
100ml taco sauce
½ butternut pumpkin, cut into chunks
1 rib celery, chopped
1 red capsicum, chopped roughly
2 tomatoes, chopped
6 spring onions, chopped
100g toasted flaked almonds
100g sultanas or raisins
50g pumpkin seeds (pepitas)

2 tablespoons stock, extra
2 tablespoons taco sauce, extra
½ cup parsley, chopped

Method

Heat the olive oil and add the chilli, garlic and onions. Sauté for 5 minutes, or until softened but not brown. Add the rice and stir to coat. Add the pumpkin chunks (skin may be left on as an option) and stir well.

Add half a cup of stock, stirring well and simmering until all the liquid has been absorbed. Then add the celery and tomatoes with the next addition of stock. Continue adding stock until all the liquid has been absorbed, stirring thoroughly after each addition. When all the stock has been absorbed, remove the pan from the heat and add the capsicum, chopped spring onions, flaked almonds, sultanas and pepitas with the remaining extra stock and taco sauce. Stir very well and serve immediately garnished with the parsley.

Chilli con Carne Risotto

Chilli con Carne is the most famous of all the Texan/Mexican dishes and was instrumental in the development of Tex-Mex cuisine. This version produces a lovely rich, meaty stew that clings to the grains of rice in perfect harmony. Serve this as a robust main course and your guests will be very satisfied.

Ingredients

750g minced beef
1 teaspoon red chilli, minced
2 cloves garlic, minced
1 teaspoon cumin
1 teaspoon cinnamon
2 tablespoons olive oil
500ml tomato purée
2 tablespoons tomato paste
salt and pepper

1 tablespoon olive oil
1 onion, chopped
400g arborio rice
200ml red wine
700ml rich beef stock, simmering
200ml mild taco sauce
2 tomatoes, chopped
2 x 400g can red kidney beans
$\frac{1}{2}$ cup parsley, chopped

70ml stock, extra
$\frac{1}{2}$ cup sour cream
$\frac{1}{2}$ cup coriander leaves, chopped

Method

First make the chilli con carne. Heat the olive oil and add the cinnamon, cumin, chilli and garlic. Sauté until softened but not browned, about 2 minutes. Add the minced beef and sauté over high heat quickly, separating the mince quickly to avoid it cooking together. When the meat has changed colour, add the tomato paste and purée, and reduce the heat to a simmer. Cook this mixture slowly until it is thick and full of flavour, about 1 hour. Season to taste with salt and pepper. Set aside.

Heat the remaining olive oil and add the onion. Sauté until the onion is softened, then add the rice and stir to coat. Add the red wine and simmer until the liquid has evaporated and the rice mixture appears quite dry.

Begin adding the stock, half a cup at a time, stirring well between each addition. When half the stock has been absorbed, add the chilli con carne mixture, kidney beans, taco sauce and tomatoes. Stir well, then add the next addition of stock, continuing in this way until all the stock has been absorbed. Remove the pan from the heat and add the remaining stock and parsley, and stir well.

Serve the risotto in individual bowls, garnished with a dollop of sour cream and a handful of coriander leaves.

Risotto en Cazuela

This rich and slow-cooked traditional dish is usually prepared with rabbit. I find chicken a much more popular substitute—choose skinless breast fillets for a delicious main course. The addition of orange juice and zest encourages an amazingly different flavour, one I think you will find delightful.

Ingredients

3 chicken breast fillets, skin removed
1 teaspoon paprika
1 tablespoon olive oil
2 cloves garlic, minced

1 onion, finely chopped
400g arborio rice
150ml red wine
800ml rich chicken stock, simmering
200ml taco sauce
2 tablespoons tomato paste
2 large tomatoes, chopped
juice and zest of 1 orange
1 green capsicum, sliced

150ml sour cream
orange zest, extra
½ cup parsley, chopped

Method

Coat the chicken with paprika. Heat the olive oil in a large saucepan and sauté the garlic for 1 minute. Add the chicken pieces and cook until golden on both sides. Remove from the pan and cut into strips.

In the same pan, add the onion and cook until softened. Add the rice and stir well to coat. Add the wine and simmer until the liquid has been absorbed and the alcohol has evaporated. Add the chicken strips, taco sauce, tomato paste, tomatoes, juice and zest of 1 orange and green capsicum strips and stir thoroughly to combine. When the liquid has been absorbed, add the stock half a cup at a time, stirring well after each addition. Continue until the stock has all been added.

When all the stock has been absorbed, remove the pan from the heat and serve in individual bowls, garnished with sour cream, extra orange zest and parsley.

Caribbean Pantry

The cuisine of the Caribbean is influenced by the climate, of course, but also by the diverse cultural influences in its long and interesting history. Native fruits and vegetables such as guava, cassava, sweet potatoes and cashew fruit were supplemented with the introduction by Columbus of such 'exotica' as tomatoes, corn and chillies. The geographical position of the Caribbean also made fish, shellfish and water fowl a very important part of this diet.

The recipes I have chosen borrow heavily on flavour combinations of this tropical region and I must stress that I have used artistic license to make them workable for cooking with rice. Most of the vegetables should be available at markets or ethnic food stores and there are certainly speciality food importers who will be able to help with any that are difficult to find.

I hope you enjoy this diverse journey into the flavours of this lesser-known cuisine.

Parsley Peanut Risotto with Deep Fried Leeks

This combination may sound unusual, but the flavours of this risotto are wonderful. Rich and full of flavour and texture, I like to serve this risotto as part of a light lunch, with a salad to add freshness.

Ingredients

2 tablespoons peanut oil
8 shallots, chopped
3 cloves garlic, minced
½ Spanish onion, chopped
2cm piece fresh ginger, peeled and finely chopped, or
2 teaspoons ground ginger
1 small red chilli, finely minced

400g arborio rice
200ml white wine
800ml light vegetable or chicken stock, simmering
1 cup chunky peanut butter
1 cup raw peanuts, toasted (in oven, microwave
or sauté pan)
1 cup parsley, chopped

1 tablespoon lime juice
2 tablespoons extra stock
2 leeks, cut into fine strips and deep fried until crisp

Method

Heat the peanut oil and sauté the shallots, garlic, onion, ginger and chilli until the onions are softened. Add the rice and stir to coat, making sure all grains are shiny. Add the wine and simmer to absorb the liquid while the alcohol evaporates, stirring all the time.

Begin adding the stock, half a cup at a time, stirring well between each addition. When half the stock has been absorbed, add the peanut butter, toasted peanuts and parsley. Continue adding stock as before, stirring thoroughly.

When all the stock has been absorbed, remove the pan from the heat and add the lime juice and extra stock. Stir vigorously.

Garnish with the deep fried (and drained) leeks, mounded into little 'nests', and serve immediately.

West Indian Sweet Potato Risotto with Spiced Sour Cream

(photographed on page 91)

The traditional West Indian vegetable of choice here would be a calabaza. However, because it is almost impossible to source, I have substituted a combination of sweet potato and butternut pumpkin which together contribute a sweet, smooth texture with a glorious colour and a velvety consistency. The spiced cream is an unusual and delightful garnish.

Ingredients

1 kg sweet potato
½ kg butternut pumpkin

2 tablespoons olive oil
2 onions, finely chopped
1 carrot, finely chopped
2 ribs celery, finely chopped
2 cloves garlic, minced
1 teaspoon green curry paste
400g arborio rice
200ml white wine
800ml chicken stock
2 bay leaves

150g sour or thickened cream
¼ teaspoon cinnamon
¼ teaspoon ground coriander
¼ teaspoon ground cumin
½ bunch chives, finely chopped

Method

Peel and chop the pumpkin and sweet potato, reserving 200g of each and slicing into matchsticks for later. Place the remainder in a saucepan and cover with water. Bring to the boil and simmer for 30 minutes until both vegetables are tender. Drain, mash and set aside.

In a large saucepan, heat the olive oil and add the onions, carrots, celery, garlic and green curry paste, and reserved raw pumpkin and sweet potato, and sauté until the onions are softened, about 10 minutes.

Add the rice and stir to coat, making sure all the grains have a shiny surface and appear opaque. Add the wine and allow the liquid to be absorbed while the alcohol is evaporated. Add the bay leaves, mashed pumpkin/sweet potato mixture and the first addition of stock. Stir the risotto vigorously while allowing the liquid to be absorbed, and when the mixture becomes dry, add the next addition of stock. Continue in this way until all the stock has been incorporated, then remove the saucepan from the heat.

In a small bowl, whisk the cream with the spices. To serve, remove the bay leaves, then mound the risotto in individual bowls and garnish with a generous dollop of spiced cream and a shower of chopped chives.

Spiced Tomato and Snapper Risotto

Snapper is Nicaragua's most popular fish and turns up in all sorts of preparations. It marries so beautifully with the flavours of this dish that, although I experimented with other fishes, I couldn't match the flavour combination of snapper and spicy tomato. For a delicious garnish, serve this risotto with a dollop of coconut-flavoured sour cream.

Ingredients

700g snapper fillets, boned and diced
2 tablespoons Cajun spice
2 tablespoons cornmeal (polenta)
2 tablespoons olive oil

1 tablespoon olive oil
1 large Spanish onion, chopped
2 cloves garlic, minced

400g arborio rice
200ml white wine
700ml fish/vegetable stock, simmering
4 large tomatoes, finely chopped
2 tablespoons tomato paste
1-2 jalapeño chillies, finely chopped

1 tablespoon butter, optional
3 tablespoons sour cream
2 tablespoons toasted coconut
½ cup chopped flat leaf parsley

Method

Mix the cajun spice and cornmeal together, and toss the fish in this mixture until well coated. Heat the olive oil and cook the fish until the flesh is opaque and the coating is fragrant. Set aside.

In a separate saucepan, heat the remaining olive oil and sauté the Spanish onion and garlic until softened. Add the rice and stir to coat. Add the wine and simmer until the liquid has been absorbed. Add the first ladle of stock and stir well. Add the tomatoes, tomato paste and jalapeño chillies, and combine. When the liquid has been absorbed, continue adding stock, half a cup at a time, stirring well after each addition and allowing all the liquid to be absorbed before the next addition of stock is added.

When all the stock has been added, return the fish and all its juices to the risotto and combine gently. Add the butter and mix well.

Serve in individual bowls, garnished with a dollop of sour cream and fresh herbs. Serve immediately.

Note

To make the coconut cream, toast the coconut in the microwave until golden (about 1-2 minutes), then mix with sour cream.

Risotto of Garlic Swordfish with Raisins and Pine Nuts

What a fragrant main course this is! Swordfish is a wonderful choice because it has no fishy odour or taste and marries beautifully with garlic. The pine nuts and raisins add texture and flavour and make this a more elegant choice.

Ingredients

500g swordfish fillets
5 cloves garlic, minced
2 tablespoons olive oil

1 tablespoon olive oil
1 rib celery, chopped
1 onion, chopped
400g arborio rice
100ml white wine
900ml vegetable stock, simmering
1 cup chopped flat leaf parsley
2 handfuls baby spinach
4 tablespoons raisins
4 tablespoons pine nuts, toasted

2 tablespoons stock, extra
1 finely diced tomato
1 lemon, cut into wedges

Method

Brush the fillets of swordfish with oil and spread with garlic. Place in an oiled baking dish and bake uncovered at 230°C for 8 minutes until flesh is opaque and flakes easily. Set aside.

Meanwhile, make the risotto. Heat the olive oil and add the onion and celery, sauté until softened. Add the arborio rice and stir to coat. Add the white wine and simmer until the liquid has been absorbed. Begin adding the stock, half a cup at a time, stirring well after each addition. When adding the final portion of stock, add the parsley, baby spinach, raisins and pine nuts. Combine gently and remove from the heat.

Add the remaining hot stock and stir well to combine. Serve risotto over fillets of swordfish, garnished with a small mound of freshly diced tomatoes and one lemon wedge.

Tropical Chicken Risotto

This risotto is full of light, tropical flavours of the Caribbean. Coconut, pineapple and mango combine with chicken to create a perfect summer lunch risotto. Serve a salad of mixed lettuces garnished with peanuts for a perfect accompaniment. I have suggested using breast fillets of chicken for convenience. However, if preferred, a whole roast chicken may be used.

Ingredients

3 skinless breast fillets, pounded
salt and freshly ground pepper
2 tablespoons butter
1 tablespoon marmalade

2 tablespoons olive oil
1 teaspoon fresh grated ginger
6 shallots, finely diced
1 Spanish (red) onion
2 cloves garlic

400g arborio rice
100ml white wine
600ml chicken stock, simmering
300ml coconut milk, hot
1 handful baby spinach

1 cup finely diced firm mango
1 cup finely diced firm pineapple
2 tablespoons toasted coconut
2 tablespoons chives, chopped

Method

Season the breasts with salt and pepper and place in an oiled baking dish. Melt the butter and mix with the marmalade. Brush this marinade over the chicken and bake uncovered for 15 minutes at 210°C Remove from the oven and keep warm.

Heat the olive oil and saute the ginger, shallots, onion and garlic. Add the rice and stir to coat. Add the wine and allow to simmer for a moment or two until the liquid has been absorbed. Begin adding the stock, half a cup at a time, stirring well after each addition. When half the liquid has been absorbed, dice the chicken and add to the risotto with the next addition of stock. When all the stock has been absorbed, continue adding the coconut milk in the same fashion.

When all stock and coconut milk have been added, remove the pan from the heat and add the mango and pineapple and stir to combine. Serve in individual bowls, garnished with toasted coconut and chives and serve immediately.

Rum-spiked Veal Risotto with Pineapple Salsa

This is quite an unusual recipe. The rum flavour is not obvious in the finished dish but certainly contributes flavour. Serve the pineapple salsa as an interesting garnish for a really tropical flavour. Plantains should be available from ethnic market stalls or shops catering for Caribbean or Latin American cuisine.

Ingredients

600g veal, cubed
¾ cup dark rum
¼ cup fresh pineapple juice (from salsa)
2 tablespoons olive oil
3 cloves garlic, minced
3 tablespoons lime juice
salt and pepper to taste
2 tablespoons olive oil
1 bunch spring onions, chopped
2 semi-ripe green bananas
400g arborio rice
200ml white wine
800ml chicken stock
½ cup parsley, chopped
For The Salsa:
1 small pineapple
½ red onion, finely diced
½ red capsicum, finely diced
½ cup fresh coriander leaves, chopped
2 tablespoons fresh mint leaves, chopped
2 tablespoons lime juice
salt and ground pepper to taste

Method

Place the veal in a baking dish with the rum, pineapple juice, olive oil, garlic, lime juice and salt and pepper to taste. Marinate for 2 hours, then drain most of the liquid and grill the veal, turning frequently until the meat is almost cooked through. Set aside.

Heat the olive oil and sauté the spring onions until softened. Add the peeled and diced bananas and cook for 3 minutes. Add the rice and stir to coat. Add the wine and simmer until the liquid is absorbed, stirring all the time.

Begin adding chicken stock, half a cup at a time, stirring well after each addition and allowing all the liquid to be absorbed before adding the next quantity of stock. When half the stock has been absorbed, add the cooked veal cubes and their juices and combine gently.

Continue simmering the risotto, stirring well and adding stock as necessary, until all the stock has been added and absorbed. Remove the pan from the heat and stir through the parsley.

Serve in individual bowls garnished with pineapple salsa.

To make the salsa, cut away the skin of the pineapple and cut the flesh into tiny dice. Mix with all the remaining ingredients and serve immediately on top of the risotto or on the side.

Fire and Spice Risotto

This rich, spicy and full-of-flavour risotto showcases typical flavours of the Caribbean. Loads of garlic, ginger, coriander, cumin, tumeric and lime juice combine to flavour the beef with a wonderful mix of ingredients. Make this a main course dish, and serve with some palate refreshers such as a tomato and cucumber salad and some yoghurt.

Ingredients

800g skirt steak or cubed goulash beef
4 tablespoons olive oil
8 cloves garlic, minced
3 teaspoons fresh grated ginger
1 bunch of spring onions, chopped
½ cup parsley, chopped
½ cup coriander, chopped
2 small red chillies, minced
2 teaspoons cumin
2 teaspoons ground coriander
2 teaspoons tumeric

1 tablespoon olive oil
400g arborio rice
100ml red wine
100ml sherry
750ml beef stock, simmering
2 tomatoes, chopped

2 tablespoons lime juice
¼ cup parsley, chopped
1 finely sliced onion, deep fried
⅓ cup yoghurt
extra parsley

Method

Heat 4 tablespoons olive oil and add all the ingredients in the first group, except the beef. Sauté gently until the vegetables have softened and the mixture is aromatic. Add the beef and continue to sauté until the beef changes colour, about 5 minutes. Set aside.

In a separate saucepan, heat the remaining tablespoon olive oil and add the arborio rice. Stir to coat, then add the red wine and sherry, simmering until the liquid has been absorbed. Begin to add the beef stock, half a cup at a time, stirring well after each addition and allowing each to be absorbed before adding the next quantity. When one quarter of the stock has been added, add the chopped tomatoes and the beef mixture including all the liquid and spices, and continue to cook until the liquid has been absorbed. Continue adding stock in the usual manner until all the stock has been added and absorbed.

Remove the pan from the heat and add the lime juice and parsley, stirring well. Serve in individual bowls, garnished with a little yoghurt, a mound of fried onions and a sprinkling of parsley.

Note

To deep fry onions, heat some oil and add the finely sliced onions, allowing them to cook until a deep golden brown. Remove with a slotted spoon and allow to drain on absorbent paper. Place in a microwave for 1 minute on 'high' to crisp further if desired, then pile onto risotto.

Risotto with Low Fat Ricotta and Herbs

Fresh ricotta cheese provides an amazingly silky, rich flavour and texture while contributing almost no fat. You will not believe this risotto is so light! Add any fresh herbs you prefer—dill marries particularly well with the flavour of the ricotta. Make sure you buy the fresh ricotta that drains in a colander, not the whipped variety available in tubs in the supermarket.

Ingredients

1 teaspoon olive oil
1 clove garlic, minced
1 leek, white part only and washed and finely chopped
2 tablespoons fresh dill or other preferred herb

400g arborio rice
100ml white wine
900ml light vegetable stock, simmering

300g fresh ricotta or to taste
4 tablespoons fresh dill or other preferred herb

1 tablespoon yoghurt
6 tablespoons fresh ricotta
1 tablespoon stock, extra
4 tablespoons fresh parsley, finely chopped
salt and pepper to taste

Method

Heat the olive oil in a non-stick saucepan and sauté the garlic and leek until softened.

Add the rice and stir to coat then add white wine. Stir continuously until the liquid has absorbed, then begin adding the hot stock, half a cup at a time and stirring well after each addition. When half the stock has been absorbed, add the ricotta cheese and herbs and continue stirring, adding stock and allowing each addition to be absorbed before adding the next quantity. Add salt and pepper to taste.

When all the stock has been added, remove the saucepan from the heat immediately, add the yoghurt and remaining stock and stir vigorously. Serve in individual bowls garnished with remaining ricotta sprinkled on top and finish with finely chopped fresh herbs.

Variation

I love this risotto with roasted peppers and goat cheese. Cut and seed the peppers and cut into large slices. Place these under a hot grill and cook until the skins are blackened. Place the black peppers into a double thickness plastic bag and seal, allowing them to steam. Set aside for thirty minutes then when cool enough to handle, simply peel off the skins. Chop the capsicum flesh and add to the risotto with the last addition of stock. When adding the yoghurt, mix 50g chopped goat cheese and proceed. (The heat of the risotto will assist the goat cheese in melting).

Risotto of Cherry Tomatoes

(photographed on page 105)

This is a beautiful dish. Light, fresh and full of flavour and it looks pretty too—it is hard to believe that this dish is low in fat. Make it at the height of summer when cherry tomatoes are cheap and plentiful. If possible, purchase a variety of colours to add interest to your meal.

Ingredients

3 punnets of assorted cherry tomatoes

1 teaspoon olive oil
1 clove garlic, minced
1 Spanish onion, finely chopped

400g arborio rice
200ml white wine
850ml light vegetable stock, simmering

20 fresh basil leaves
½ cup parsley, chopped
2 tablespoons dill, chopped

1 tablespoon low fat yoghurt
1 tablespoon parmesan cheese, grated
1 tablespoon stock, extra

Method

Reserve approximately 1 punnet of the cherry tomatoes for later use.

Heat the olive oil in a non-stick saucepan and sauté the garlic and Spanish onion until softened. Add the rice and stir to coat. Add the wine and cook over a high heat, allowing it to be absorbed by the rice.

When the wine has disappeared, add the first addition of stock and all but the reserved cherry tomatoes. Stir well. Continue adding the stock in the usual manner—half a cup at a time and stirring well after each addition.

Meanwhile, finely dice the reserved punnet of cherry tomatoes and reserve for garnish

When adding the final quantity of stock, add all the herbs. Cook for 2 minutes further until most of the liquid has been absorbed then remove the saucepan from the heat.

Add the yoghurt, parmesan cheese and remaining 1 tablespoon stock and stir well. Garnish each bowl with a generous pile of finely diced (or halved) cherry tomatoes and serve.

Variation

To make a more hearty version, add 500g diced chicken when sautéing the garlic and onion. Proceed with the recipe as specified above.

Risotto Niçoise

This risotto is my tribute to that wonderful 'Salad Niçoise'. Full of tasty, low fat flavours, this risotto will become a favourite of yours too.

Ingredients

500g fresh tuna steaks
½ cup light fish stock

1 teaspoon olive oil
4 cloves garlic, minced
1 brown onion, chopped

400g arborio rice
150ml white wine
800ml vegetable or fish stock, simmering
200g green beans, trimmed
2 Pontiac potatoes, peeled and diced

2 tablespoons stock, extra
1 tablespoon parmesan cheese
½ cup Kalamata olives, pitted and finely chopped
½ cup parsley, chopped

Method

Heat the fish stock and add the tuna steaks. Poach gently for 5 minutes then remove the fish from the liquid and dice. Reserve the fish liquid.

Heat the olive oil and sauté the garlic and onion. Add the rice and stir to coat. Add the wine and allow the liquid to be absorbed. Add the cubed potatoes and combine.

Begin adding the stock, half a cup at a time and stirring well after each addition.

When half the stock has been absorbed, add the green beans. Continue adding the stock in the usual manner until all has been added and absorbed. Add the poaching liquid and stir well while it is being absorbed.

Remove the pan from the heat and add the extra stock and parmesan cheese. Stir vigorously to combine then garnish with parsley and olives. Serve immediately.

Variation

Although not at all traditional, I like to make a Seafood Risotto Niciose. Instead of using tuna, select 500g assorted seafood such as calamari, prawns, scallops and white fish cut into chunks. Poach in the fish stock for three minutes, then proceed with the recipe as above.

Risotto Primavera

The term 'primavera' refers to a pretty mix of spring vegetables, contributing fresh colour and flavour. The vegetables called for are available all year round and I make this lovely version whenever I want a taste of spring. This risotto makes a perfect entrée because it is light and fresh-tasting.

Ingredients

2 ribs celery, finely chopped
2 medium carrots, finely chopped
2 medium zucchini, finely chopped
half bunch of asparagus, finely chopped (optional)
½ cup parsley, chopped

1 teaspoon olive oil
1 clove garlic, minced
1 small brown onion, finely chopped

400g arborio rice
200ml white wine
850ml vegetable of chicken stock, simmering

2 ears of fresh corn
1 tablespoon yoghurt
1 tablespoon parmesan
1 tablespoon stock, extra
½ cup parsley, chopped

Method

Place all the finely chopped vegetables in a bowl and mix well.

Heat the olive oil and sauté the garlic and onion until softened. Add half the vegetable mixture and stir well to combine (reserve remaining vegetables).

Add the rice and stir to coat. Add the wine and stir well while allowing the liquid to absorb.

When all the wine has been absorbed, begin adding the stock, half a cup at a time and stirring well after each addition. Continue adding the stock in the usual manner, stirring regularly.

When adding the last addition of stock, add the remaining vegetables and stir well.

When all the stock has been added and absorbed, remove the risotto from the heat and add the yoghurt, parmesan and extra stock.

Cut the fresh corn off the ears of corn and mix into the risotto.

Serve in individual bowls garnished with parsley.

Variation

The addition of 500g of lean lamb will make this dish more hearty—I love the combination of fresh vegetables and lamb. Sauté the lamb with the garlic and proceed as above.

Risotto Desserts

*T*his is a relatively new and inspiring way of looking at risotto. While it may come as a surprise, arborio rice cooked by the traditional method produces a rice that is tender, creamy and perfect for dessert. The addition of fruit, sugar syrups, coconut and liquor combine to create a satisfying and quite nutritious end to a meal. Obviously we cannot use a savoury stock as the liquid in a sweet risotto, so these recipes all contain variations of sugar syrups, fruit juices and nectars. You may like to keep a little sugar syrup in your refrigerator for whenever you want to prepare a sweet risotto quickly—sugar syrups have an unlimited shelf life.

*M*any cultures have embraced the use of rice in desserts that are well accepted as 'comfort foods'. Thai glutinous rice pudding, Arabic concoctions featuring honey, nuts and spice and English rice pudding all demonstrate the ease with which rice adopts sweet flavours. While I had no precedent for the creation of risotto desserts, these recipes simply evolved from my love of all things 'rice'; and once I began thinking of sweet rice, the ideas tumbled forth, faster than I could type.

*A*ll these recipes have been tried on unsuspecting friends who have never eaten a sweet risotto, and the general consensus is that this is a lovely (although unexplored) way of serving risotto. When contemplating a risotto dessert, make sure that the rest of your meal is light and not too filling—I have found that a lovely main course salad or fish leaves my guests comfortable but still ready, willing and able to end their meal with one of the treats within this chapter.

*T*he first couple of recipes in this chapter will probably appeal to the child in your family, but the others are very definitely adult tastes. Enjoy this new journey into the unknown!

Coconut Pistachio Risotto

(photographed on page 112)

This risotto has slightly Asian overtones. The coconut flavour is both delicate and robust, while coconut milk provides a creamy textured end to a meal. Some tropical fruit would make a fresh and light accompaniment.

Ingredients

2 tablespoons butter
4 tablespoons shredded or desiccated coconut
4 tablespoons pistachio nut kernels
4 tablespoons 'palm' sugar or brown sugar

400g arborio rice
800ml coconut milk
200ml water

2 tablespoons cream
1 tablespoon golden syrup, brown sugar or honey
toasted coconut shavings and roasted pistachio nuts

Method

Mix the coconut milk and water together and bring to a simmer.

In a saucepan, heat the butter until melted. Add the coconut, pistachio kernels and sugar, and sauté until the coconut is golden and the sugar melted.

Add the rice and stir to coat. When all the butter has been absorbed, add 1 cup of coconut milk mixture and stir well. When the rice has absorbed the liquid and is quite dry, add the next addition of coconut milk mixture. Continue in this fashion until all the coconut milk has been absorbed and the rice is tender.

Add the cream and golden syrup or honey and stir thoroughly. Serve small portions in individual bowls and garnish with toasted coconut shavings and chopped pistachio nuts with berry ice cream.

Champagne and Strawberry Risotto

(photographed on page 113)

What a romantic combination! Champagne and strawberries have long been paired together with delightful results and this recipe is no exception. Use fresh, sweet flavoured strawberries with good colour. The quality of champagne is your choice— use one that appeals to your own tastes.

Ingredients

2 tablespoons butter
200g well flavoured strawberries, chopped
400g arborio rice
400ml champagne
600ml water
150g sugar
200g well flavoured strawberries
30ml strawberry syrup or liquor

Method

Mix the water and sugar together in a small saucepan and bring to the boil. Simmer gently while you begin the risotto.

Heat the butter and sauté the chopped strawberries until softened.

Add the rice and stir to coat, cooking for a moment or two until the butter has been absorbed by the rice. Add the champagne and simmer until there is no alcoholic aroma wafting from the pan, and the rice has absorbed the liquid.

Begin to add the sugar syrup, 1 cup at a time, stirring well after each addition and allowing the liquid to be absorbed before the next addition.

When all the sugar syrup has been absorbed, remove the pan from the heat. Add the remaining strawberries and strawberry syrup and stir well. Serve immediately over savionie biscuits, with a little extra syrup spooned over the top.

Citrus Risotto

Although desserts made with rice tend to be a little heavy, this version is full of flavours that are light, bright and bouncy. The combination of citrus zest, juice and pulp will make this a special favourite of yours too.

Ingredients

2 tablespoons butter
4 tablespoons sugar
zest of 1 lime
zest of 1 lemon
zest of 1 orange

400g arborio rice
100ml white wine
800ml orange juice, simmering

2 oranges, segmented and chopped
juice of 1 lemon
juice of 1 lime
2 tablespoons demerara sugar*
50g toasted flaked almonds

available from Asian food stores

Method

In a saucepan, add the butter, sugar and all the zests. Stir well and sauté until the mixture is bubbling and fragrant.

Add the rice, stir well and cook for 2 minutes.

Add the white wine and mix well, allowing all the alcohol to evaporate and the liquid to be absorbed by the rice. Add 1 cup of orange juice and stir while the rice simmers in the juice. When the rice begins to look a little dry, add the next cup of juice and stir well again. Continue in this fashion until all the juice has been added and absorbed and the rice is tender.

Stir through the orange segments, juice of lemon and lime and demerara sugar, and garnish with toasted almonds.

Fig and Rhubarb Risotto

There is no fruit quite as exotic as figs, and whether fresh or dried, they provide a lovely flavour to any recipe. I believe rhubarb is a much under-rated fruit (a vegetable, actually) and this combination works very well. It would be a perfect end to a winter's dinner, in front of an open fire with a long, cosy evening ahead.

Ingredients

2 tablespoons butter
8 ribs (sticks) rhubarb, red part only
10 dried figs, halved

400g arborio rice
400ml orange juice
600ml water
150g sugar

1 tablespoon mascarpone cheese
4-6 fresh figs
1 tablespoon brown sugar

Method

Mix the orange juice, water and sugar together, and simmer for 10 minutes.

Wash and slice the rhubarb into 2cm pieces. Heat the butter and add the rhubarb and figs, and sauté for 3 minutes.

Add the rice and stir to coat. When the rice is shiny, begin adding the syrup/juice mixture, 1 cup at a time. Stir well to incorporate the ingredients. When the liquid has been absorbed and the rice is a little dry, add the next addition of syrup and stir well.

Continue in this fashion until all the liquid has been absorbed and the rice is tender.

Add the mascarpone cheese and stir well.

Cut the fresh figs in half and sprinkle a little brown sugar on each cut surface. Grill the fruit, sugar side up until caramelised, about 2 minutes, then serve atop the risotto in individual bowls.

Mixed Berry Risotto

This intensely-coloured risotto makes a startling end to a meal. It reminds me of a summer pudding, both in colour and flavour, and is lovely with a dollop of fresh cream. Do not make this unless berries are in season—they are too expensive out of season and the flavours are not as intense.

Ingredients

2 tablespoons butter
1 teaspoon cinnamon

400g arborio rice
200ml light red wine
600ml water
150g sugar
2 punnets raspberries

1 punnet blueberries
1 punnet blackberries
1 punnet raspberries

100ml thick cream
2 tablespoons brown sugar

Method

In a saucepan, heat the water, sugar and raspberries and simmer for 5 minutes. Purée until smooth and keep hot.

Heat the butter and sauté with the cinnamon for a moment or two. Add the rice and stir well. Add the red wine and simmer until the liquid has been absorbed.

Begin adding the raspberry syrup, 1 cup at a time, stirring well after each addition and allowing the liquid to be absorbed before adding more syrup.

With the last addition of syrup, add the washed blueberries, blackberries and raspberries, and stir gently so as not to bruise the fruit.

Serve warm in individual bowls garnished with a dollop of cream and a sprinkle of brown sugar.

Risotto of Caramelised Apples and Pears

This risotto reminds me of 'Tarte Tartin'. Warm apples and caramel are a wonderful combination and marry perfectly with rice. The maple syrup in this recipe really sets off the autumn flavours of the fruits.

Ingredients

3 tablespoons butter
3 tablespoons sugar
2 tablespoons maple syrup
2 Golden Delicious apples
1 Beurre Bosc (brown) pear
1 teaspoon cinnamon

1 tablespoon butter
400g arborio rice
100ml white wine
600ml apple juice
300ml water

4 tablespoons sour cream
½ teaspoon cinnamon
1 red apple, course grated and tossed with lemon juice

Method

In a non-stick frypan, heat the butter, sugar and maple syrup, and boil until syrupy, about 3 minutes.

Add the peeled, cored and sliced fruit and cinnamon, and toss in the butter mixture. Simmer the fruit until caramelised and golden, about 10-15 minutes. Set aside.

Mix the apple juice and water together and heat to simmering.

In a saucepan, melt the butter and add the rice, stirring to coat. Allow the rice to absorb the butter then add the wine, simmering until the alcohol has evaporated and the rice is dry.

Begin to add the simmering apple water, 1 cup at a time, stirring well after each addition and allowing the liquid to be absorbed before adding more apple water.

When half the apple water has been absorbed, add the caramelised apples and pears and stir well to distribute. Continue adding the apple water as before until it has all been absorbed.

Remove the pan from the heat and add half the sour cream. Stir well to distribute.

Serve in individual bowls, garnished with a small dollop of sour cream, a sprinkling of cinnamon and some grated apple.

Risotto of Nectarine, Basil and Pine Nut

We all know and love fresh basil as an indispensable herb in savoury cooking, but here, it stars as a flavouring for our sweet risotto. Do not attempt to use dried basil instead of fresh here, as it would overpower the delicate fruit flavour.

Ingredients

2 tablespoons butter
4 firm nectarines, sliced
1 teaspoon balsamic vinegar
4 fresh basil leaves, finely shredded

400g arborio rice
100ml white wine
400ml apricot nectar
400ml water
100ml orange juice
2 tablespoons brown sugar

3 tablespoons pine nuts
3 tablespoons creme fraîche (light sour cream)
3 basil leaves, finely shredded

Method

In a saucepan, heat the butter and add the nectarine slices and basil leaves. Sauté until the fruit is golden, then add the balsamic vinegar. Stir well, then remove the nectarines and set aside.

Combine the water, apricot nectar and orange juice and heat to simmering.

To the remaining hot butter, add the arborio rice and stir well to coat. Add the white wine and simmer until the liquid has been absorbed and the alcohol has evaporated.

Add 1 cup of juice mixture and the brown sugar and stir well, allowing the rice to simmer until all the liquid has been absorbed, before adding the next quantity of juice.

When all the juice has been added and absorbed, remove the risotto from the heat and serve in individual bowls, with nectarine mixture over top garnished with toasted pine nuts, creme fraîche and finely shredded basil leaves.

Note

To toast pine nuts, cook on 'high' in the microwave for 1 minute, check for colour and stir. Continue to cook on 'high' until desired colour is achieved. Alternatively, toss in a non-stick pan over a medium heat, just until golden.

Leftover Risotto

Once you have eaten a freshly prepared risotto, you will forever be spoiled by the tenderness and texture of this Northern Italian staple and will turn your nose up at reheated risotto.

What, then, can we do with leftovers?

While I doubt you will ever have leftover risotto (my family and friends eat every last grain from the pan), it is very useful to have some ideas for turning leftover risotto into a whole new dish that really works beautifully.

I have found these recipes so popular, that I intentionally make more risotto than I need, so that I will have some left over to create one of these tasty offerings.

Make sure you have allowed risotto to become cold before attempting one of these suggestions.

Arrancini or Suppli

These little crumbed croquettes are a favourite in my house. Use any cold leftover risotto and shape tablespoons of risotto into ovals. If making arrancini, poke a little cube of mozzarella cheese into the centre of each croquette. If making suppli, no filling is necessary.

When you have formed all the risotto into croquettes, dip them into beaten egg and then breadcrumbs, and chill until ready to fry.

Heat your oil to 170°C, then deep fry the risotto croquettes until golden brown. Drain on absorbent paper then serve hot.

For a more substantial snack, serve alongside a rich Napoli sauce.

Al Salto (Risotto Cakes)

Risotto al Salto is a traditional Italian way of using up leftover risotto. Simply put, the cold risotto mixture is flattened into thin patties about 10cm across, then fried in butter or oil until crisp. Turn and cook the second side, then serve. If you are anxious about the risotto cakes holding together, add a beaten egg to your cold risotto and mix thoroughly before shaping. As with arrancini, any flavoured risotto can be used, with Saffron Risotto being the most traditional. I like to serve these as part of a formal main course, topped with stir-fried vegetables and then fish, chicken or beef.

As a Quiche or Pie Crust

This is a wonderful idea. I came across it quite by chance one day when I found I had no pastry for a quiche. I used some leftover tomato risotto pressed into the base of the pie dish and, expecting a disaster, I was thrilled to have created a masterpiece.

Again, use any leftover risotto and press firmly into a buttered pie/quiche dish. Bake at 200°C for 10 minutes, then cool. Now proceed with your quiche filling, bake according to your recipe and enjoy!

Risotto in Soup

Risotto is a welcome addition to any soup, whether a broth, a thick chunky soup or a cream soup. The addition of risotto will contribute extra flavour and texture and any variety can be used.

Remember to add the risotto while the soup is heating, so that the risotto will disperse evenly.

I also like to add leftover risotto to a frittata (Italian omelette). Simply whisk leftover risotto into beaten eggs, add your other flavourings and cook your frittata as you would an omelette.

Instead of turning the frittata once the underside is cooked, place your frypan under a grill and cook the top until sizzling and firm.

Index